UNDERSTANDING
LANGUAGE

Donald Fairbairn

UNDERSTANDING
LANGUAGE

A Guide for Beginning Students of
Greek & Latin

THE CATHOLIC UNIVERSITY OF AMERICA PRESS
Washington, D. C.

The paper used in this publication meets the minimum
requirements of American National Standards for Information
Science—Permanence of Paper for Printed Library Materials,
ANSI Z39.48-1984.

∞

Library of Congress Cataloging-in-Publication Data

Fairbairn, Donald.

Understanding language : a guide for beginning students of
Greek and Latin / Donald Fairbairn.

p. cm.

Includes index.

ISBN 978-0-8132-1866-3 (pbk. : alk. paper)

1. Greek language—Grammar, Comparative—Latin.

2. Latin language—Grammar, Comparative—Greek.

3. Greek language—Textbooks for foreign speakers—English.

4. Latin language—Textbooks for foreign speakers—English.

I. Title.

PA111.F35 2011

485—dc22   2010050051

In memory of Dr. William H. F. Kuykendall—
my Hebrew teacher, my sounding board in Greek
and Latin, and the first person ever to call me
a linguist

Contents

Tables and Figures

Acknowledgments

My conviction that a book comparing Greek and Latin might be useful to beginning students emerged through conversations with my Latin students at Erskine Theological Seminary in 2007–2008. Future groups of my Latin students in 2008–2009 and my Greek students in 2009–2010 were the test audiences for early drafts of the manuscript, and I acknowledge with fondness the role these students played in helping me produce and revise the material. Some of these students are named (by first name only) in the imaginary conversations sprinkled throughout the book.

I would like to thank my friend Michael Johnstone, whose Ph.D. in linguistics from Cambridge and vast experience in multiple Indo-European languages (as well as a few languages from other families) made him the ideal person to critique the manuscript for linguistic accuracy. His suggestions led to many important revisions.

I would like to thank Dr. Carole Burnett, editor of the Fathers of the Church series, and Dr. John Dunlap, classics professor at Santa Clara University. Their enthusiasm about this project went a long way toward securing the book's publication.

I would like to thank Dr. David McGonagle and the editorial staff at the Catholic University of America Press for encouragement, constructive criticism, attention to details, and kindness in seeing the manuscript through acquisition and production.

Despite the attention of these sharp-eyed critics and editors, linguistic and grammatical deficiencies doubtless remain in the book. I take complete responsibility for these deficiencies and invite criticism from the professors and students who use the book.

Preface: For Teachers

It is well-known among teachers that the hardest thing about learning any foreign language is breaking out of the mental box in which people unconsciously live, a box that tells us subliminally that the way we express ideas in our own language is the best or even the only way to express those ideas. Even though this fact is widely acknowledged, many Anglophone students of Greek and Latin are nevertheless taught to relate what they are learning directly back to English. They are told that this tense in Latin does the work of those two tenses in English, or this case in Greek works like that prepositional phrase in English. Of course, this is a natural way to teach English speakers a classical language, but my work with beginning language students has convinced me that this approach aggravates the problem we already have—treating our own language's ways of expressing ideas as the standard. Students who are following this approach remain in their English boxes longer than necessary, and they get frustrated when Greek and Latin do not work the way they are supposed to (that is, the way English works).

Furthermore, teaching Greek and Latin this way is especially problematic for today's students, because these students do not usually have a good theoretical understanding of English grammar. Students know how to use English, but they cannot usually articulate the way English works. Most of them cannot diagram sentences, identify parts of speech (which are now often called "word classes"), or explain syntax correctly. One can rail against this fact, one can long for the days when students had a better theoretical command of English grammar, but one can hardly escape the admission that it *is* a fact. So in order to relate Greek or Latin grammar back to English, teachers must first spend a fair bit of time explaining English grammar and its accompanying terminology to the students. I suggest that this common practice winds up simply creating confusion, because the teachers are explaining one unknown—Greek or Latin grammar—in light of something else—English grammar—that may still be largely unknown to the students. (The Latins had a proverb to describe this—*obscurum per obscurius*—explaining something obscure through something even more obscure.) The result is a great deal of frustration for both the teachers and the students.

Teaching Greek or Latin with reference to English, however, does not merely create confusion and frustration. This approach also delays the process of learning to appreciate Greek or Latin for its own sake, learning—if you will—to think in that language. What could be a one-step process (learning how Greek or Latin works on its own terms) becomes a three-step process— first, learning how to articulate the workings of English grammar, then learning to understand Latin or Greek grammar in light of English, and then trying to understand the classical language's grammar on its own terms. Because of these problems, I suggest that instead of constantly forcing students to relate Latin or Greek to English, it would be better to help them from the beginning to understand the way the classical languages work on their own terms.

One might object that this would be too complicated for students, but I am convinced that it is not as hard as it seems. In many cases, what makes learning Greek and Latin difficult is the difficulty of English. Admittedly, there are ways in which the classical languages are quite complex, but there are other ways in which they have an elegant simplicity and an internal coherence that are lost when one tries to relate them to the complexity of English. After all, English as we know it emerged from a somewhat abrupt collision in the eleventh and twelfth centuries between two rather different languages—Anglo-Saxon (strongly influenced by Old German and the Scandinavian languages) and French (strongly influenced by Latin and more indirectly by Greek). A language that results from such a collision is bound to have a complex grammar in which two historical streams sit uncomfortably beside each other, and English does. Thus, I believe that understanding Greek and Latin on their own terms may actually be easier than trying to relate them back to English. Accordingly, this book begins not with English grammar, but with the big-picture idea that different languages can express the same concepts in different ways. Then it turns to the functional question of what languages have to accomplish to enable speakers and writers to communicate well. What do nouns have to do? What do verbs have to do? How can words and phrases be combined to express complex ideas? In the process of describing what the parts of a language must accomplish, this book introduces common grammatical terminology. I try to keep the terminology to a minimum, and I always define the terminology with reference to Greek and Latin, not with reference to English. I also include a bit of historical information about the evolution of the Indo-European languages from the pre-literary parent language to Greek and Latin and then to the modern European languages. I include this information because I am convinced that working from the big picture to the details enables a student to learn and remember the details more easily. For example, I have found that my students can remember the specific uses of the ablative case in Latin more easily if they have first learned that there are eight basic kinds of relations between words, that these eight relations are handled in Indo-European languages by either cases or prepositional phrases or both, and that the basic idea of the ablative is "separation" or "distinction."

In keeping with this goal of focusing on the big picture, I always explain both Greek and Latin grammatical patterns and include illustrations from both languages. Indeed, in many cases the illustrations come from the same passage of the same text (the Greek New Testament and its Latin translation in the Vulgate Bible), and I discuss similarities and differences in the ways the two languages express the same idea. Accordingly, although your students are taking only Greek or Latin (at least for now), I encourage you, the teacher, to require students to read and pay attention to the book's discussions of both Greek and Latin. The more clearly one sees the way different languages accomplish the same tasks, the easier it is to grasp the way a specific language works. It is no secret that having studied multiple languages enables one to learn another foreign language more easily. In some ways, thinking through this book will give the student some of the conceptual benefits of studying two closely-related languages, Greek and Latin, even though that student is actually studying only one of them now.

I suggest that you, the teacher, might adopt one of two basic plans for your students to follow in reading this book. The first plan would be for students to read parts 1, 2, and 3 at the beginning of their study of Greek or Latin and then to read part 4 after they have completed the basics of morphology. The second plan would be for students to read only part 1 at the beginning, and then to read part 2 when they are introduced to the case system, part 3 when they come to verb forms beyond the present indicative, and part 4 when they have completed the basics of morphology. With either reading plan (or some other one that works well with the way your primary textbook is arranged), I think it will help students to have a big-picture view of what nouns and verbs must accomplish before they learn how to build the various forms and what the specific usages of those forms are.

I have found that this approach to teaching Greek and Latin has helped my own students considerably. Fairly often, when I explained a point of Latin grammar in connection with the Greek grammar that my beginning Latin students supposedly already knew, the students commented, "I wish we had known this when we took Greek!" In fact, my experience with my own students was what initially convinced me that I needed to write this book. I am happy to share this approach with you, and I hope it will be similarly helpful for your students. As you and your students use this book in connection with your language textbook, I hope that the process of teaching/learning Greek or Latin will be less frustrating and more enjoyable both for you and for them.

Introduction: For Students

Greek and Latin are normally referred to as the "classical languages" because they were the languages of the two great ancient cultures—Greece and Rome—that helped to forge the modern Western world. Because of the vast impact those cultures have had on Western society, and because of the equally great influence of those languages on the modern languages of the West, the study of Greek and Latin has long held an important place in the curricula of Western schools and universities. In the latter half of the twentieth century, that prominence waned substantially as education began to branch out and to focus on other cultures and languages of the world. Such expansion is of course important, but still one cannot get away from the influence of the Greek and Roman worlds upon our modern Western civilizations and our languages. Therefore, Greek and Latin continue to hold an important place in the world of scholarship, and many students continue to have the privilege (although they may consider it more a chore than a privilege) of being exposed to those languages.

Students today study Greek and Latin in a variety of contexts. Seminarians preparing for Christian ministry learn Greek to study the Septuagint, the New Testament, or the documents of the Eastern Christian Church. Some of them, especially Roman Catholic seminarians, also learn Latin in order to read the Vulgate Bible and other documents of the Western Christian Church. Undergraduate and graduate students studying the history of the ancient, Byzantine, or medieval civilizations must learn Greek and Latin to read their source materials. Some undergraduates, as well as high school students at classical schools, study Greek and/or Latin to gain exposure to the roots of Western civilization. Other undergraduates study Greek and/or Latin to help prepare for careers in medicine, law, or the sciences, since most of the technical vocabulary of these fields is derived from the classical languages. Some high-schoolers study Latin to improve their English vocabulary, and many home-schooled students do the same. This book should be helpful to students who are studying Greek and/or Latin in any of those contexts.

This book should prove useful whether students seek to study Jewish and Christian documents or the documents of pre-Christian Greece or Rome. Contrary to what some scholars thought two hundred years ago, so-called "*koine* Greek" and "ecclesiastical Latin" are not different languages from classical Greek and Latin. Christian writers did have some specialized vocabulary, and their writing reflected a later stage in the development of Greek or Latin, but they were not speaking and writing in a tongue that would have been foreign to the classical world. So whether a student's purpose is to read pagan, Christian, or Jewish material, whether one is studying *koine* Greek or classical Greek, whether one is interested in ecclesiastical Latin or classical Latin, the way the languages work is not dramatically different.

The Purpose of This Book

As you, a beginning student of Greek or Latin, pick up this book, you need to recognize right away that it is a supplement to a Latin or Greek textbook, not an actual textbook itself. It contains none of the forms or words that you will have to memorize. It has no practice sentences. In fact, it contains relatively few Greek or Latin words. Instead, this is a book about language. In order to understand Greek, Latin, or any other foreign language on its own terms, one needs to understand language in general. That is, one needs to have a basic grasp of the different ways that a language *could* function, so that one can then recognize and appreciate the way a given language *does* function. This book seeks to give you—a beginning student—enough familiarity with language in general that you will understand what the various parts of a language have to accomplish in order for speakers and writers to communicate well in that language. Building on this foundation, the book also seeks to explain to you how Greek and Latin accomplish the tasks of language. The concepts this book presents will not be a substitute for the hard work of learning forms, memorizing vocabulary, and practicing. Nevertheless, I hope the book will make that hard work less frustrating and more rewarding sooner than might have otherwise been the case. So this is a book about language, with special reference to Greek and Latin.

At this point, a question naturally arises: Why should this book focus on both Greek and Latin when you are probably studying only one of them (at least for now)? Why should you have to read about a language you are not learning at the moment? I suggest that your acquisition of Greek *or* Latin will be faster and more enjoyable if you understand something of the way *both* of them work. The reason I believe this is that I am convinced that a big-picture approach to language will help you. If it is true that understanding what language (in general) must accomplish will help you learn any language, then it is also true that understanding how several languages (especially several closely related languages) accomplish the same purpose will help you grasp and appreciate the workings of the language you are learning. Thus, reading a book that deals with how both Greek and Latin work will help improve your grasp of the one you are trying to learn now. The two classical languages are similar in many ways, and yet each has its own style and its own peculiar way of going about things. Giving some attention to both of them will help you notice and understand the nuances of the one you are trying to learn.

Of course, it is also possible that gaining some exposure to both of the classical languages while you study one of them will have another result—it may lead you to decide to study the other one as well. The benefits of learning one of these languages are great (and in chapter 2, I will discuss some of those benefits), but the advantages of learning both are even greater. To know both Greek and Latin is to gain a privileged view of the intellectual history of the West—in religion, technical sciences, medicine, law, and government. These languages may not be popular today (Chinese and Arabic are replacing them as the preferred languages to learn, just as Russian and German were preferred a generation ago, and French and Spanish before that), but their influence upon us is vast. The fifth-century B.C. Greek philosopher Socrates urged his students, γνῶθι σεαυτόν [gnōthi seauton], "know yourself." For a modern Westerner, to know oneself is much easier if one knows Greek and Latin. If even a handful of you who read this book because you have to take Greek *or* Latin decide you want to take Greek *and* Latin, it will have been well worth discussing both languages in the same book.

A Book for Beginning Students, by a Fellow Student

Most books that deal with both Greek and Latin are written by experts in linguistics, and such books are usually intended primarily for other experts. As you already know, however, this book is intended not for specialists, but for you, a beginning student. It is also important for you to recognize that I, the author, am not a professional linguist, and thus not an "expert" in the classical languages. By academic training I am a scholar of the Christian Church during the first several centuries after the end of the New Testament. Most of the documents from the Church's early history were written in Greek or Latin, but I am not a professional scholar of the languages per se. Rather, I use the languages to study something else, and so when it comes to Greek and Latin, I am a more advanced fellow student, not an "expert." Why then am I—rather than a professional linguist—the one writing this book?

The simplest answer to this question is that a fellow student can often help other students better than an expert can, because the expert may have forgotten the questions the students are asking. In the introduction to his *Reflections on the Psalms*, C. S. Lewis offers an apology for why he—who is not a specialist in the ancient world that produced the Hebrew Psalms—should write such a book. Lewis's memorable explanation goes like this:

It often happens that two schoolboys can solve difficulties in their work for one another better than the master can. When you took the problem to a master, as we all remember, he was very likely to explain what you understood already, to add a great deal of information which you didn't want, and say nothing at all about the thing that was puzzling you. I have watched this from both sides of the net; for when, as a teacher myself, I have tried to answer questions brought to me by pupils, I have sometimes, after a minute, seen that expression settle down on their faces which assured me that they were suffering exactly the same frustration which I had suffered from my own teachers. The fellow-pupil can help more than the master because he knows less. The difficulty we want him to explain is one he has recently met. The expert met it so long ago that he has forgotten. He sees the whole subject, by now, in such a different light that he cannot conceive what is really troubling the pupil; he sees a dozen other difficulties which ought to be troubling him but aren't.[1]

If one may apply Lewis's principle to languages, the expert linguists are so thoroughly at home in the world of grammar that they are sometimes unable to help the students to whom that world is completely foreign. They may have forgotten what it was like not to know the terminology, the lingo by which they explain the workings of languages, and so they may have little sympathy for—or ability to communicate with—the students who do not understand that terminology. In contrast to the experts, a fellow student like me may still be able to identify with your struggles to learn Greek or Latin, and so I may be better able to help you.

Closely related to the fact that I am a fellow student rather than a linguistic expert is the fact that I am an amateur, in the classical sense of that word. In English, the word "amateur" is normally used as a synonym for "untrained"—as opposed to "professional," which to our ears is synonymous with "accomplished" or "competent." This is not the way the word "amateur" has always been used, however. In Latin, the word came from the root meaning "to love," and an amateur was someone who did something out of love, rather than out of the desire for money or gain. To the Greeks and Romans, being an amateur was a higher calling than being a professional, since doing something because one loved it was considered nobler than doing something because one could get money by it. When it comes to languages, I am an amateur in that classical sense of the word. I

1. C. S. Lewis, *Reflections on the Psalms* (San Diego: Harcourt Brace Jovanovich, 1958), 1–2.

love languages. They fascinate me. I marvel at the possibilities different languages afford for expressing great ideas. Because of my love for languages, I have been paying close attention for several decades to the way a number of languages work, and as a result of that attention, I have recognized a great deal about what languages can accomplish and how they do so. The fact that I have learned this through observation, rather than through academic training per se, may mean that I can explain it to you in a less technical and more comprehensible way than could a linguist who learned the same things (and much more, of course!) through more detailed study. Furthermore, of the languages I have studied (English, French, German, Russian, Greek, Latin, and Hebrew), Greek is my favorite, with Latin ranking a close second. I love the way these two languages work, and perhaps I will be able to convey to you some of my enthusiasm.

In brief, then, the reason I think I can help you learn Greek or Latin through this book is that I have a deep love for languages, but I still look at them with a student's eye, rather than with the eye of a professional linguist. I hope that my experience with and observations about Greek and Latin will make your own efforts to learn one or the other of them be more enjoyable and successful than they would have been otherwise.

The Format of this Book

Part 1 of this book is entitled "Getting Started," and in this part I try to help you overcome two potential barriers that could make it hard for you to learn Greek or Latin. The first barrier, which pertains to learning any foreign language, is the mistaken belief that the way we express ideas in English is the only way to do so. In chapter 1 I draw illustrations from several modern languages in order to show that there are various ways to express a given idea; there is no single standard that all languages must follow. The second barrier pertains specifically to Greek and Latin, and it is the idea that there is no point in studying a "dead" language. In chapter 2 I discuss some of the many ways in which studying Greek and Latin is valuable, even if no one speaks the ancient versions of these two languages today. Then in chapter 3 I introduce you to the building blocks of language, thus giving you some of the terminology you will need to know to learn Greek or Latin.

The remaining parts of the book deal in some detail with the different ways of putting words together into sentences in Greek and Latin. Part 2 deals with nouns, adjectives, pronouns, and articles (words that correspond to "the," "a," and "an" in English). The functioning of these words constitutes the place where Greek and Latin differ most widely from English, so such words are a good place to start in showing how different languages communicate the same ideas in different ways. Part 3 deals with verbs, which are seemingly the most complicated part of Greek or Latin grammar, but I suggest that Greek and Latin verbs have an elegant simplicity about them that is lost in English. Part 4 of the book is concerned with putting sentences together, and here again, Greek and Latin work quite differently from English. Again, I hope to enhance your appreciation for the elegance of Greek and Latin sentence structure.

Beginning in chapter 3 of the book, I introduce and explain the basic grammatical terms that you will need to know in order to learn Greek or Latin. Each time I introduce a new term, I write it in **boldface** type, and at the end of each chapter, I include a list of the important terms explained in that chapter, along with a brief definition of each term (not as complete as the discussion of the term in the chapter itself). Thus, you can use the initial discussion in the text to learn each term and the list of definitions at the end of each chapter to review terms. You can also use the book's index to locate the discussion of a given term if you need to refresh your memory.

Furthermore, at many points in the book, I offer illustrations of the concepts I discuss. These illustrations are not a substitute for the more detailed examples and practice sentences of your Greek or Latin textbook, but they should help you to understand the ideas before you see specific examples in your own study of the language. I draw these illustrations from my own experience in several modern languages and from my own reading of Greek and Latin literature. Accordingly, the Greek and Latin examples come from Christian literature (primarily the New Testament), although again, the grammatical concepts I am illustrating apply in classical Greek or Latin, as well. When the illustrations involve quoting Greek words and phrases, the Greek words are both presented in the Greek alphabet and transliterated into the Latin alphabet (the one we use in English, as well). This mode of presentation means that if you are studying only Latin, and not learning the Greek alphabet, you can still read and understand the Greek illustrations.

Your teacher may ask you to read most or all of this book at the beginning of your formal study of Greek or Latin. If so, you should have a good overview of how the classical language works, and that overview should make the various details easier for you to learn. Conversely, your teacher may prefer to have you read only part 1 at the beginning of your study, and then read parts 2, 3, and 4 at appropriate points during your first year, when you begin to study the grammatical material I discuss in those parts. I hope that, whichever plan you follow for reading this book, it should equip you well to learn the language, and learning it should be less cumbersome and frustrating than it might otherwise have been.

PART 1 **GETTING STARTED**

1

LEARNING A FOREIGN LANGUAGE

The Bad News and the Good News

The Bad News: Languages Are Not Codes

Early in Thomas Hardy's last novel, *Jude the Obscure*, published in 1896, the title character catches a glimpse of the great university city Christminster (which, in Hardy's fictional world, corresponds to Oxford) and is consumed by the desire to become a scholar. Upon discovering that he will have to learn Greek and Latin to do so, Jude orders some textbooks for the classical languages and prepares to decipher them. Hardy tells the reader:

Ever since his first ecstasy or vision of Christminster and its possibilities, Jude had meditated much and curiously on the probable sort of process that was involved in turning the expressions of one language into those of another. He concluded that a grammar of the required tongue would contain, primarily, a rule, prescription, or clue of the nature of a secret cipher, which, once known, would enable him by merely applying it, to change at will all words of his own speech into those of the foreign one.[1]

When the packet of textbooks arrives and Jude eagerly opens the Latin grammar that is on top, he is devastated. Hardy writes, "He learnt for the first time that there was no law of transmutation, as in his innocence he supposed (there was, in some degree, but the grammarian did not recognize it), but that every

1. Thomas Hardy, *Jude the Obscure*, Bantam Classic Edition (New York: Bantam Books, 1981), 32.

3

word in both Latin and Greek was to be individually commit-ted to memory at the cost of years of plodding."[2] At this point, Jude throws the book down in despair and sulks for some time. Hardy continues: "What brains they must have in Christmin-ster and the great schools, he presently thought, to learn words one by one up to tens of thousands! There were no brains in his head equal to this business; and as the little sun-rays continued to stream in through his hat at him, he wished he had never seen a book, that he might never see another, and that he had never been born."[3]

Thus begins Jude's brief, unhappy relationship to the halls of academia. While most people who start the study of Greek and Latin are not quite as naïve as Jude was, many of us have very little idea of what awaits us as we embark on the journey toward learning one or both of the classical languages. Thus, finding out what is involved in studying Greek and Latin may be nearly as crushing a blow for many of us as it was for poor Jude. In fact, the bad news is that Jude did not know the half of it, because simply learning words one by one is only the beginning of the difficulties that await the student of Greek or Latin. The greater problem is coming to grips with the hundreds of different forms that a single Greek or Latin verb can take and the dozen or so forms each noun can take. One must learn how to recognize each of these forms and how the forms are used to indicate rela-tions between words. This is considerably more daunting than simply learning, for example, that "human being" in Latin is *homo,* that in Greek "human being" is ἄνθρωπος [*anthrōpos*], and that there is no code enabling one to produce these two words from the English word "man" or the phrase "human being."

Let us think a bit more about Jude's humorous idea that languages were like codes or ciphers. Behind that supposition lay another belief—not articulated or even considered, but still present—that there cannot really be more than one way to ex-press ideas. The way Jude was used to expressing himself—that is, the way people express themselves in English—was the only way he had ever experienced, and thus it was the only way of

2. Ibid.   3. Ibid., 33.

expressing ideas he could conceive of. So when he tried to imagine what another language might entail, the only thing he could come up with was something like a code, a sort of trick in which one letter stands for another, or symbols stand for the letters of the alphabet. Again, most of us are not as naïve as Jude, but we probably share more in common with him than we like to admit.

We assume—whether we realize it or not—that English is more absolute than it is, that the way of relating words to one another in English is the best or the only way to do so. We assume consciously or unconsciously that English is the standard. As a result, we subconsciously assume that learning another language is primarily about learning the new words that correspond to our English words. This unarticulated assumption creates two major problems for us when we start learning another language. First, there is nothing absolute or even superior about the way English relates words to one another to form ideas. The way we do it is not the only way, or even the best way. It is simply one way to do so. Second, in many cases the words of one language do not correspond exactly to another language. The words overlap, but they do not always match exactly. I would like to illustrate both of these problems with a few examples.

As an illustration of the first problem, consider the following English sentence: "I want you to do this for me." Believe it or not, this is not the most common way to convey this simple idea. Most of the European languages express this idea in a way that, if we were to translate it into English, would be more like this: "I want that you should do this for me." Now, we can understand that latter sentence, and in fact, you may have heard a native French or Spanish speaker say something like this in English. Nevertheless, that latter sentence should sound quite odd to your ears, because it is not the best way to convey that idea in English. If you step back from your English way of thinking, though, you should be able to recognize that there is nothing inherently better about saying "I want you to do this for me," versus saying "I want that you should do this for me." Some languages (like ours) insist that the first is correct; other languages work in such a way that the second is correct.

As another example, consider this sentence: "I would like

a cup of coffee." In English, the relation between the cup and the liquid in the cup is expressed by the word "of." Other languages, however, have different ways of expressing that relation. It is possible that you have heard a native Hebrew speaker say, in English, "I would like a cup-coffee." If so, that probably sounded very strange to you, and the strangeness comes from the fact that Hebrew conveys that relation between words in a different way from English. Speakers of other languages might say the equivalent of "a cup with coffee," and I have even heard a native Russian speaker say "a coffee cup" when he meant "a cup of coffee." This last phrase—"a coffee cup"—is an especially good illustration of the point I am making here, because it is actually correct English, but it does not mean the same thing as "a cup of coffee." In some cases, relating words to one another in a way that is not correct in a certain language means that you will sound funny but still be understood correctly—when you say "a cup with coffee" for example. In other cases, you will be misunderstood—when you say "a coffee cup" rather than "a cup of coffee." Conversely, if you are hearing or reading a foreign language and hear/see something like "a coffee cup" but think it means "a cup of coffee," you will misunderstand. Studying another language involves learning how that language relates words to one another. If you do not learn those relations of words well enough, sometimes you will *fail to understand* (that is, you will not have any idea what is being communicated), and at other times you will *misunderstand* (that is, you will think you have understood what is being communicated but in actuality you have understood incorrectly).

One more example of this first problem should suffice. Consider this English sentence: "The book is on the table." In English, if we want to speak of several, rather than one, then obviously we say "books" instead of "book." (That is, we change the form of the word "book" from singular to plural.) If we want to refer to the past, rather than the present, we say "was" rather than "is." (That is, we change the form of the verb "to be" from present tense to past tense.) There are some languages (like Greek and Latin) that have far more forms for each word than English does, but there are other languages that have even fewer forms than English. In Indonesian, for example, the way one says "books" is simply to repeat the word: "book book." The way one refers to the past is simply to give a time reference while leaving the word "is" in the same form. So in order to say, "The books were on the table," one would actually have to say the equivalent of "The book book is previously on the table." A language that works like this is cumbersome in some respects, but it is simple and therefore easy to learn once one recognizes that it does not work anything like English. In contrast, a language with many different forms—like Greek or Latin—is efficient and precise, but harder to learn.

Now let us consider some examples of the second problem: the fact that words do not correspond exactly from language to language. Suppose you want to order a rare steak at a restaurant in France. If you simply look up the word "rare" in your French dictionary, you will find that it is *bleu*. If you then order your steak *bleu*, you will be in for a bit of a shock when the food arrives. In France, the word for rare is *bleu* because a rare steak actually is blue in color on the inside. It has been cooked so little that it is not even red; it is still purplish. To get a steak that is equivalent to "rare" in America, you would have to order it *bien cuit* or "well done," and it would be virtually impossible to get a steak that is well done by American standards. The words for "rare" and "well done" do not correspond in English and French because the cultures behind those languages have different ideas about what constitutes an appropriate length of time to cook a steak.

Let us take another example. Two of the most commonly used words in English are "get" and "put." The first of these is amazingly versatile; it can be used to refer to everything from asking for directions ("How do you get there from here?"), to growing ("Your children sure are getting big"), to giving something to another person ("Please get me a Kleenex"). In contrast, there is no such catch-all word in German; a person has to use one of dozens of much more limited, precise words, depending on which particular nuance of "get" is needed in a given situation. Similarly, in Russian you cannot simply "put" a book on a table. You have to "lay" it or "stand" it on the table. The greater precision of Russian and German means that they have no words corresponding to the general words "get" and "put" in English. Again, the words do not always match exactly from one language to another.

As a final example of this problem, take the following English words and phrases: "packed," "granular," "corn," "spring," and "champagne powder." If you are like most English speakers, you probably cannot recognize anything that these words have in common, but if you are a skiing enthusiast (or even if you are not, but you have lived in Colorado), you can probably recognize fairly quickly that all of these words are used to describe certain kinds of snow conditions at a ski resort. Within a particular subculture, a number of ordinary English words are used in a different way from their normal usage in the language as a whole, so much so that most English speakers cannot recognize how they are being used. If this can happen *within* a language, then it can happen all the more *between* languages. Words are not cosmic absolutes that are always used the same way in all languages and all situations. Therefore, the words of one language do not match up perfectly with those of another language, and indeed the way certain people speaking one language use a given word may not be comprehensible to everyone who speaks the same language. Thus, studying a language involves learning the concepts behind the words and learning the different ways words are used by different speakers/writers and in different situations within the same language.

From these examples, we can recognize that the bad news about learning a foreign language is even worse than poor Jude realized when he despaired over the difficulty of mastering Greek and Latin. Neither the ways words are used (that is, the "meaning" each word has in each situation) nor the ways words relate to one another (that is, how they are combined to express the ideas one needs to articulate) are the same from one language to another. In some cases, these word usages and ways of relating words to one another line up a lot more closely than in others. This is why, for example, it is much easier for an English speaker to learn French than to learn Chinese. French is one of the most closely related languages to English, but Chinese and English are about as completely unrelated as is possible, given that all languages on earth have some similarities. In all cases, however, there are significant differences in the way languages function, and when one compares Greek and Latin to English, these differences are considerable, a fact that makes the two classical languages hard for English speakers to learn. There is no getting around this fact, and we do not do ourselves any favors if we try to ignore it. We need to recognize up front that Greek and Latin are challenging, difficult languages for English speakers. This, in a nutshell, is the bad news.

The Good News: Not Knowing English Grammar Is Not Necessarily a Problem

On the other hand, we should also recognize up front that the bad news I have just described is also, ironically, good news. Because Greek and Latin work so differently from English, the fact that most students today cannot articulate the workings of English grammar should not actually hurt them too much. Of course, this claim is perhaps in opposition to what you have heard. You may have heard people say that you cannot learn Greek or Latin grammar until you know English grammar. Many students of Greek and Latin bemoan their lack of knowledge of English grammar and assume this is why they struggle, and certainly many teachers attribute their students' difficulties with the classical languages to an insufficient grounding in English grammar on the part of those students. Nevertheless, an inability to articulate English grammar may not mean that you will struggle with Greek or Latin, for two reasons.

First, I suspect that students like you actually do know English grammar better than you are given credit for. After all, English is your language. You have been hearing and speaking it your whole life, and in most cases, you can probably identify the correct and incorrect ways to say something. For example, even though you may say, "me and Paul are going to lunch," the chances are good that you actually know the correct way to express that idea is "Paul and I are going to lunch." Even though you say, "just between you and I," you might be able to guess that "just between you and me" is correct. On the rare occasions when someone actually says, "I couldn't care less," then if you think about it for a while, you can probably recognize why that sentence makes more sense than the typical expression, "I could care less." I believe that most students actually do intuitively recognize the difference between "correct" or "formal" English and the colloquial English we usually speak. Thus, most students actually do know English grammar intuitively. They just do not have the theoretical and terminological underpinnings to articulate why a certain way of saying something is correct in formal English and another way is incorrect. If I am right about this, it is not actually true that today's students do not know English grammar, and therefore it is not necessarily true that today's students will struggle in Latin or Greek.

A second reason an inability to articulate English grammar may not hurt you is that *English* grammar is not what you are trying to learn right now. What you are trying to learn is Latin or Greek grammar, and in some ways, if you start with a clean slate because you have not drunk too deeply from the well of technical English grammatical terminology, you will be better off. Your mind will be less cluttered with preconceived notions that every language ought to work like English, and you may be better able to grasp how Greek and Latin do work early in the process of learning those languages. In fact, the terminology that we use today to describe English grammar was originally developed by the Greeks and Romans to describe their own languages. Thus it should not be surprising that in some cases, this terminology fits the classical languages better than it fits English, and so for someone who is encountering that terminology for the first time, it may actually be easier to learn the terms as they apply to the languages for which they were designed, rather than to learn them as they apply to a later language that they may not fit as well.

For example, you may have heard that in order to have a complete sentence, one must have a subject (the person, place, or thing one is writing about) and a verb (a word describing the action that person, place, or thing does, or the action that happens to that person, place, or thing, or the state of being in which that person, place, or thing exists). This is true in English, but it is actually a modification of a much more basic and universal grammatical principle. The actual principle is that a sentence must include a subject and a predicate (something one says about the subject). In English (unlike Greek, Latin, and many other languages), a verb is a necessary part of a predicate. So in English, and almost exclusively in English, the "rule" that one must have a subject and a verb holds true. Thus, if a student starts with English grammar and learns this rule, then the student will have to unlearn the rule as soon as he gets to Greek or Latin. In contrast, if one starts with the general principle that one must have a subject and a predicate, and then learns that in Greek and Latin one can sometimes construct a predicate without a verb, then the student will be less confused and ultimately gain more precision in his understanding of the grammatical principle involved.

Please do not misunderstand me here. As you study Greek or Latin you will have to learn a lot of grammatical terminology, much of which also applies (perhaps in different ways) to English. So if you do know English grammatical terminology well, you are in good shape as long as you can recognize that what you learned about English grammar is an application of general principles to a specific language, and that in Greek or Latin you will need to work with the general principles rather than with the specific applications you have learned before. If you do not yet know grammatical terminology well, however, it will be easier for you to learn it as it applies to Greek and Latin than to go through the medium of English. So if you, like most students today, are not adept at articulating the way English functions grammatically, that should not be a reason for you to despair about your ability to learn Greek or Latin. You can learn the grammatical terminology just as well in relation to another language as you could have learned it in relation to English, and in fact, the terminology may make more sense to you in relation to Greek or Latin than it would in relation to English, French, or German. This, I suggest, is the good news that goes along with the bad news that other languages (especially Greek and Latin) are so different from English.

This chapter has dealt not specifically with Greek and Latin, but more generally with learning any foreign language. One must overcome the initial barrier of subconsciously assuming that English is the standard, assuming that learning the new language is primarily a matter of learning new words. In addition to that general barrier, however, there is another important barrier related specifically to the study of Greek and Latin. These languages, we hear, are dead languages. Why should we study languages that no one speaks anymore? Even if you can successfully learn Greek or Latin, why would you want to do so? This is the question I will address in the following chapter.

2

STUDYING A DEAD LANGUAGE

Why Bother?

When you ask why one should study Greek or Latin, you may be thinking that the only reason you are doing so is because you have to. If this is the case, then you should remember that the reason someone is making you study the language is because that someone is convinced that there is some purpose in learning it. Why, then, should one learn a "dead" language like Latin or Greek? When we ask this question, we should immediately recognize that, unlike many other ancient languages, Greek and Latin are not dead in the sense of having vanished from civilization and being accessible only to archaeologists and professional linguists. Both Greek and Latin have been with us continuously since their emergence, and it is worth giving a brief history of the two languages.

Greek emerged as a written language about 1200 B.C., and of course it existed as a spoken language prior to that time. To oversimplify somewhat, the three dialects of ancient Greek that are most interesting to contemporary students are Ionic, Attic, and *koine*. The first of these can be described as the coming-of-age of the Greek language in the ninth and eighth centuries B.C., and this was the dialect in which Greek was first written using an alphabetic script. It is of interest partly because it is the dialect of Homer's *Iliad* and *Odyssey*. Attic Greek is the dialect spoken in Athens during the heyday of the Greek Republic, from about the sixth through fourth centuries B.C. It is the dialect in which much of the great Greek drama was written, as well as the early Greek philosophical and scientific writings. This is the Greek of Sophocles, Plato, and Aristotle. *Koine* ("common") Greek is the name given to the everyday dialect that emerged in the Greek world after the conquests of Alexander the Great in the late fourth century B.C. It became the trade language of the Near East and was the dialect in which the New Testament was written.

During the Byzantine period (from the fourth through fifteenth centuries A.D.), many writers sought return to the style of Attic Greek, rather than using the more commonly spoken *koine* Greek. In fact, even in the modern period, many Greeks attempted to preserve the archaic forms of earlier Greek, and it was not until the late twentieth century that such efforts were largely abandoned and written Greek began to follow the conventions of spoken Greek very closely. Thus, one may delineate Ionic, Attic, *koine*, Byzantine, and modern forms of Greek, among others. Sometimes students and teachers refer to the various Greek dialects from before the Christian era as "classical Greek" and contrast this with both "*koine* Greek" and "modern Greek," but this distinction is artificial. Greek has had a continuous history as both a spoken and a written language.

Latin emerged as a written language about 500 B.C., and of course it too existed as a spoken language prior to that time. The classical period of the language is usually regarded as having run from the early first century B.C. to the end of the second century A.D. (within this time period, some scholars speak of an earlier "golden age" and a later "silver age"); and Latin from the second century A.D. to the breakup of the Roman Empire in the fifth century is called "late Latin." During the period of late Latin, the language was increasingly used by Christian authors; therefore, many scholars distinguish between "classical" (earlier) and "ecclesiastical" (later) Latin. This distinction is somewhat artificial, but the main difference between classical and ecclesiastical Latin is that the latter has been influenced to some degree by the Hebrew of the Old Testament and the Greek of the New Testament. A significant number of Greek words and a fair number of Hebrew-style expressions came into the Latin language as Christian writers translated the Scriptures.

Latin ceased being spoken by ordinary people after about A.D. 700, as it was replaced by French, German, Spanish, Italian, Romanian, and other languages in previously Latin-speaking lands. Nevertheless, Latin has been kept alive as the language of scholarship since that time, and later versions of the scholarly language are called "Medieval Latin," "Renaissance Latin," and "neo-Latin." It was common for scholars to write and speak in Latin as late as two hundred years ago, and even today, scholars who publish editions of ancient texts sometimes write their introductions to those texts in Latin. Furthermore, Latin remained the dominant spoken language of the Roman Catholic Church long after it ceased being spoken on the streets, and it is still the primary language used in writing by Roman Catholic ecclesiastical officials.

Therefore, the only way one can refer to Greek and Latin as "dead" languages is to claim that Latin is dead because it is not an everyday language of the people any longer, and that the Greek spoken today is different enough from the Greek of Plato or Paul that it hardly qualifies as the same language. Students of Greek or Latin in schools, universities, and seminaries today are primarily (but not exclusively) interested in the ancient versions of Greek and Latin, not in modern Greek or in Latin as it is used by the Vatican today. As a result, study of these languages usually focuses on reading, not on speaking or writing, and this focus adds to the misleading impression that these are dead languages.

Even if one discards the adjective "dead," however, the question still remains: Why should we study a language that ordinary people do not speak anymore? Obviously, if one needs to speak a language, then one has to learn it well, and one will likely be fairly motivated to do so. On the other hand, if all one has to do is read literature written in that language, it is not so clear why one needs to learn it. After all, we may think that most of what we would need to read in Greek or Latin has been translated into English. This is not actually true, but a great deal of Greek and Latin literature has been translated. Furthermore, today we have access to translation programs that can give us a rough idea of what a document in another language says. Why should we go to all the trouble of learning Greek or Latin when we could just read a professional translation or use a translation program? This is an important question, because a student's success in learning a language is heavily dependent on how motivated he is at the beginning of study.

Answering this question thoroughly would take a whole book in itself, because there are many ways in which the study of Greek and Latin can be valuable. In this chapter, I would like to concentrate on three such reasons. Because of the wide variety of situations in which students study Greek and Latin, not all of these reasons will apply to all students. Nevertheless, whether you are a seminary student preparing for ministry, an undergraduate or graduate student in history, philosophy, medicine, or law, or a school student, at least one of these three benefits of studying the classical languages will apply directly to you.

Reading Greek and Latin Literature with New Eyes

First of all, studying the Greek or Latin language enables one to catch nuances in the ancient literature that translation software cannot pick up and that may even be lost in professional translations. The better we understand Greek or Latin, the better we can grasp the thought patterns and mindset of the classical world. Doing this will enable us to understand the literature of that world better, even when we are reading it in English translations. To say this another way, one reads an English translation of a Greek or Latin work differently—and more accurately— when one has studied Greek or Latin than one could if one had no exposure to those languages. Even if you never read a Greek or Latin writing that is unavailable in an English translation, and even if you never get good enough at a classical language to read a text easily without having the English translation in front of you, it will still be worth your effort to study Greek or Latin, because doing so will enhance your understanding of the texts. This is why many seminaries make ministerial students learn Greek, even though there are countless English translations of the New Testament available, or why Greek is so crucial for students of philosophy, in spite of the proliferation of translations of Plato and Aristotle, or why Latin is central to the study of Western history, even though many great texts of that history have been translated. In fact, even if you are already familiar with the literature of your field in translation, you have many surprises in store for you as you begin to learn the language in which that literature was written. Let me give you a few examples from my field, early Christian history and theology, with the recognition that one could offer comparable examples from any other field in which there is Greek or Latin literature.

The most well-known verse of the New Testament—and thus the most famous sentence ever written in Greek—is John 3:16, which reads, "For God so loved the world that he gave his only Son, that whoever believes in him should not perish but have eternal life." Generations of children have memorized this passage, and doubtless the overwhelming majority of them have understood the word "so" to mean "so much." Countless sermons and Bible lessons have focused on the vastness of God's love for the world: "He loved us so much that. . . ." Of course, it is true that God loves us "so much," and other passages of the Bible emphasize this fact, but this passage is not talking about the greatness of God's love. The Greek word οὕτως [houtōs] is not used in the sense of "so much"; it is used to mean "in such a way," or "in this manner." John 3:16 is saying that the way God loved the world was by giving his only Son, Jesus. When I taught this verse to my own son (then three years old), I taught it to him as "This is the way God loved the world." God's giving of his Son to us is the very definition of his love, not merely the result of how much he loves us. Thus, the most famous verse in the Bible appears to us with deeper significance as we begin to understand the nuances of Greek words.

Let us take another example from the New Testament, one that has to do with Greek grammar rather than Greek word usage. After his resurrection, Jesus gives his disciples the "great commission" to Christianize the world. Part of this commission, as recorded in Matthew 28:19–20, is: "Go therefore and make disciples of all nations, baptizing them in the name of the Father and of the Son and of the Holy Spirit, teaching them to observe all that I have commanded you." As Christian preachers focus on this commission, they often describe it in terms of four parallel commands: "go," "make disciples," "baptize," and "teach." Of course, there is nothing wrong with depicting the commission this way, but the relations among those four words are much more nuanced than such statements indicate. The passage actually has only one command: "make disciples." The word for "go" is in a form that suggests it is less a command than an assumption: something like "once you have gone forth, make disciples."[1] The words for "baptize" and "teach" are in forms that suggest ongoing actions as the means of fulfilling the one command to make disciples. So the great commission is not telling Christians to do four distinct things. It is primarily telling us to do one thing: to make disciples of all nations. In order to do that, we must obviously go to all nations, and the way we are to make disciples is by baptizing (initiating people into the Christian faith) and teaching (continuing to explain to them what Christian life involves). An understanding of the way the Greek verbs in this famous passage relate to one another gives Christians a deepened appreciation for the great commission.

Now consider a more complicated historical-theological example that involves both Greek and Latin. One of the great intellectual battles in Western history came during the sixteenth century over the meaning of the word "justification." This battle was part of the larger struggle within the Western Church that ultimately separated Roman Catholicism from Protestantism. The Protestant Reformers insisted on a distinction between the Latin verbs *iustificare* ("justify") and *sanctificare* ("sanctify"), with the former meaning "to declare righteous" and the latter "to make holy." These Reformers argued that God justifies sinners by grace at the beginning of Christian life when he credits the righteousness of Christ to them. In contrast, they insisted, God sanctifies Christians gradually by making them actually righteous. Roman Catholics in the sixteenth century, however, regarded these two words more or less as synonyms. Why did the two groups under-

---

1. It is true that the forms used here (an aorist participle followed by an aorist imperative) often function in Greek in the way that two linked imperatives function in English. Nevertheless, the construction here is placing its emphasis not primarily on the act of going, but mainly on the command to make disciples.

stand these words so differently? Well, in Latin there is little difference between the two words. "Righteousness" and "holiness" are synonyms, and both *iustificare* and *sanctificare* include a suffix (*-ficare*) meaning "to make." Both words were coined by the early Church (they did not exist in pre-Christian Latin) to indicate that God makes people holy or righteous, not that he declares them to be holy/righteous. (If one were going to coin a Latin word to mean "to declare righteous," then a better choice would perhaps be *iustivocare*.) So a person who was thinking in Latin would invariably understand these two words as synonyms. They *were* synonyms in Latin and always had been. The Protestant Reformers, even though they were writing and debating in Latin, were actually thinking on the basis of the Greek words in question: δικαιόω [*dikaioō*]—translated "to justify"—and ἁγιάζω [hagiazō]—translated "to sanctify." These two Greek words do not merely contain the synonymous roots for "righteous" and "holy." Rather, they also include different suffixes, and one of the great religious-linguistic questions of history is whether those different suffixes convey similar ideas or distinct ideas. Many scholars argue that the -οω [-*oō*] suffix on the verb translated "to justify" conveys the idea of "to declare," and the -αζω [-*azō*] suffix on the verb translated "to sanctify" conveys the idea of "to make." Other scholars disagree, arguing that these suffixes both convey the same idea, "to make." So if there is a difference between the Greek verbs translated "to justify" and "to sanctify," the difference comes from the different kinds of verbs they are, as determined by the different suffixes. Even though the Reformers were writing in Latin, they were basing their arguments about the difference between the words on nuances they believed were present in the Greek New Testament, nuances that were emphatically not present in the Latin New Testament, because the Latin words in question had the same suffix. It should come as no surprise, then, that the Protestant Reformers and the Roman Catholics had trouble understanding each other. The former were, so to speak, thinking in Greek (or perhaps, in accordance with their understanding of Greek, an understanding that not everyone believes is correct) but speaking in Latin, whereas the latter were thinking and speaking in Latin.

This is admittedly a complicated example, but its very complexity shows that one of the most cataclysmic conflicts in the history of the Western world was intimately tied to theological points that require a significant knowledge of Greek and Latin to understand. To return to the more general idea of this section, we read the texts more accurately once we have studied the languages in which they were written. Even if one reads Reformation-era texts only in English, studying Greek and Latin will enable one to grasp more fully why the word "justification" was so controversial, and why it was so hard for each side to understand what the other side was saying. The historical events that helped to forge the modern world appear in a new light as we learn the classical languages. What is true in the field of religion/theology is true in other fields as well—studying the classical languages enhances our grasp of the literature we need to understand in order to recognize how we in the West have become who we are.

Bringing One into Contact with the Roots of Western Civilization

Studying Greek and Latin does more, however, than merely enhance our understanding of literature written in those languages. A second, closely related benefit is that through our study of texts written in Greek and Latin, we come into contact with the world that birthed and nurtured Western civilization. Let us now consider that idea in more detail and bring other fields besides religion into the picture.

In addition to the obvious connections between the Greek and Latin worlds and the religious development of Western society, consider also that Greece was the birthplace (at least in the West) of democratic forms of government,[2] of scientific and mathematical investigation, of such literary genres as the epic poem and dramatic tragedy, and of philosophical thinking. The Greeks created our Western ideal of the perfect society,[3] gazed into the workings of geometry and astronomy in order to describe physical reality, and sought to define the relation between this present

2. The word "democracy" itself comes from two Greek words meaning "the authority of the common people."

3. "Utopia" is a Greek-based word; ironically, it means "no place."

world and the higher spiritual world of which they believed this one was a copy. Furthermore, consider that Rome gave the West the underpinnings of its legal system and a great deal of its architectural and engineering prowess. The Romans mastered the science of moving water vast distances to expand civilization into inhospitable regions and to improve hygiene, and of using concrete and stone seemingly to defy gravity, and thus to build ever-more-majestic public buildings. They also pioneered the concepts of rights belonging to individual citizens, of toleration for various religions, and of what we now call "due process" in legal matters. The contributions of Greece and Rome to the modern Western world have been immense, and even from this brief sketch, one can see that those contributions have been different. The Greeks gave us our ideals, our longing for what ought to be, whereas the Romans gave us our ability to manage, reshape, and use what is. The Greeks gave us the theoretical, the Romans the practical, and Western society has drunk deeply from both wells.

Of course, one does not need to study the languages to learn this, but when one does study Greek and Latin, one begins to see how these languages mirror the character and accomplishments of the Greek and Roman people. Greek is one of the world's most sophisticated languages—a language of nuance and subtle shades of meaning. It is thus ideal for the expression of philosophical and theological thought, as well as for the abstract or "pure" sciences like mathematics. Latin lacks some of Greek's nuance, but it is much better for making clear-cut distinctions and forming categories. It is thus well suited to law and practical technologies like architecture. This is not to say that one has to use a certain language to express certain kinds of ideas, or that being a native speaker of a certain language means one cannot go into a certain field. One's language does not determine one's thought patterns or dictate the kind of thinker one can become. At the same time, it is perhaps not a coincidence that speakers of Greek provided the great early advances in philosophy and the natural sciences, whereas speakers of Latin provided the world with its great achievements in practical engineering and law. Speaking a certain language nudges one toward a certain way of thinking and a certain kind of thought. Thus, learning

Greek and Latin does more than enable one to read texts that have helped to shape our civilization. It also places one into contact with the mindset, the genius, of Greece and of Rome, as that genius is reflected in each language.

Enriching One's Understanding of the English Language

A third benefit of studying Greek and Latin is that doing so greatly enriches our understanding of our own language. English is one of the most eclectic languages in human history, in that it has willingly borrowed words from hundreds of different languages. Nevertheless, at the most basic level almost half of all English words come from Germanic/Scandinavian words present in the Old English dialects spoken in Britain prior to A.D. 1000, and most of the others come from Latin by way of French, which began to influence the English language after the Norman Conquest of England in A.D. 1066. Among the other language families that have contributed to English vocabulary, the one that ranks next in line after the Germanic/Scandinavian tongues and the Latin/French is Greek. Quite often, the most basic, everyday words in our language come from Germanic roots, whereas slightly more exotic words come to us from Latin through French. Greek, in contrast, provides us with much of our technical and scientific vocabulary, although Latin contributes greatly here, as well.

In the previous chapter, for example, I mentioned that there is no code or formula for transforming the English phrase "human being" into the Greek word ἄνθρωπος [anthrōpos] or the Latin word homo. In fact, however, those Greek and Latin words are no strangers to us. Most of us recognize homo because we know the Latin phrase homo sapiens or "thinking man," the technical scientific term for the human species. Likewise, we know ἄνθρωπος [anthrōpos] from the technical word "anthropology," the scientific study of mankind. Indeed, the word "humanity" itself is Latin-based, from humanitas. Thus, the most basic word on this subject, "man," comes from Germanic roots, the slightly more technical word "humanity" comes from Latin, and the still more technical term "anthropology" comes from Greek (along with related words like "philanthropist").

Similarly, English often takes synonyms from its Germanic, Latin, and Greek roots to express the same idea. For example, a "guess" (from Germanic/Scandinavian roots) is a bit more ordinary than a "supposition" (from Latin), and both of these are a good deal less technical than a "hypothesis" (from Greek). The most technical term comes from Greek and the most everyday word from Germanic/Scandinavian roots, with the Latin word lying somewhere in between. The practice of culling multiple synonyms from different languages makes English a nightmare for foreigners to learn, but it gives our language a richness of vocabulary, an ability to express fine shades of meaning with its words, that is perhaps unmatched among all the world's languages. Studying Latin or Greek (or even better, both of them) enables one to grasp and appreciate more of the richness the English language possesses.

Learning Latin and/or Greek can also make the scientific and medical worlds a good deal less foreign to us. For all the bewildering complexity of surgical procedures, they basically fall into two categories: "-plasty" (such as dermatoplasty or angioplasty) and "-ectomy" (such as tonsillectomy or hysterectomy). The first category comes from the Greek word πλάσσειν [*plassein*], meaning "to form," and the second from the Greek word ἐκτομή [*ektomē*], meaning "cutting out." Surgical procedures either re-form a body part that is damaged, or they cut out something that is harmful to the body. As another example, consider the metric system. Most of us know that a millimeter is a thousandth of a meter and a centimeter is a hundredth, but we probably have trouble remembering that a decimeter is a tenth of a meter. We also know that a kilometer is one thousand meters, but we may not know that a hectometer is one hundred meters, and a dekameter is ten. How can we remember the lesser-known prefixes? By recognizing that in the metric system, the Latin words for 10, 100, and 1,000 are used to make the prefixes for the fractions (1/10, 1/100, 1/1,000), but the Greek words are used to make the prefixes for the multiples (10, 100, 1,000). Learning Greek and Latin enables us to make sense of metric units, surgical procedures, and countless other scientific terms, and when we understand where these words have come from, it makes it much easier for us to remember and use them. What is true in these fields is true in many others, as well. In *most* fields of academic study, the English technical terms derive primarily from Greek or Latin.[4]

The fact that studying the classical languages can enrich our understanding of English is perhaps the main reason high school students used to be required to study Latin (and, more rarely, Greek), and it may be a large part of the reason for the rise of private "classical" schools in the last generation or so, as Latin has become less common in public-school curricula. At the same time, high schoolers in search of higher SAT verbal scores are not the only ones who could benefit from Latin and/ or Greek. Undergraduate students in liberal arts fields at most colleges and universities have to take a foreign language, and for those who are headed to theological, medical, or scientific fields, Latin or Greek would make more sense than French or Spanish. In the case of law, the influence of the classical languages is even greater than in other fields. A vast amount of English legal terminology is taken from Latin (not just words, but phrases such as *habeas corpus, argumentum ad hominem,* or *ex post facto*), so pre-law students would do well to study that language. The fact is that, in many fields, English as we use it today is heavily influenced by Latin and Greek. The better one understands the classical languages, the better one can function in fields that depend on those languages, fields whose English vocabulary is based primarily on Greek and/or Latin.

It is often said that the discipline of learning a foreign language is valuable enough to be worth the considerable effort, even if a student is never going to speak that language regularly. This is true, and similarly the discipline of learning a "dead" language like Greek or Latin is worth the effort, even if one is not going to be a scholar who pores daily over classical texts or even a teacher of the classical languages. In this chapter, we have seen that

4. There are some exceptions, of course. In music, Italian words are the basis for most of the terms, and in literature many German words are used as technical terms.

(among other benefits) studying Greek and Latin will enrich students' understanding of the classical texts they do read (even if they read them in translation or with the help of translation software), will give students greater contact with the foundations on which Western society has been built, and will greatly enrich students' understanding of the English language, especially as it is used in professional, scientific, and technical fields. All this, of course, comes on top of the obvious benefit that studying Greek and Latin will place students into closer contact with the history of the Judeo-Christian tradition, the dominant religious tradition of the West. Greek and Latin are far from being dead. Instead, one could say that they have carried the lifeblood of Western civilization for 2,500 years. While contemporary educational theory properly emphasizes that other ideas besides Western ones deserve our attention, the importance of Greek and Latin for today's students—the heirs of Western civilization—is as great now as it ever was.

In this chapter and the previous one, we have considered two initial barriers that impede students' early efforts to learn Greek or Latin. It is now time to direct our attention to the task of language itself. What does one actually have to do to communicate well in a given language? How do Greek and Latin facilitate this task? These are the questions that will concern us for the remainder of this book, and in order to help us get started understanding them, I will turn in the next chapter to some of the basic concepts of communication.

3

THE BUILDING BLOCKS OF LANGUAGE

During one of my creative writing classes in college, the professor started a discussion with the question, "What do writers
want?" After the surprised students fumbled around a bit, the
professor answered her own question by stating, "They want to
be read." Indeed, at the most basic level, this is what communi-
cators want: writers want people to read their works; speakers
want people to listen to them. The reason for that desire, more
often than not, is that the writers and speakers believe they have
something to say that other people should want to read or hear.
In other words, they want to communicate something to their audiences, and they want the audiences to understand them and to
learn. The task of language, of course, is to facilitate such communication. In order to be understood by as many people as possible, and with as little effort on the audience's part as possible, a
speaker or writer must know how to use the language of the audience well (whether or not that is his own language). Conversely,
if a student is trying to understand a lecture or a written work in
another language, he must be sufficiently familiar with the way
that language facilitates communication in general and with the
way that particular speaker or writer uses the language.

How, then, do languages facilitate communication? In short,
they do this by the way they use words and by the way they convey the relations between the words. The basic building blocks
of communication are the words that convey the author's meaning.[1] These words have different usages (often called "mean-

1. This assertion is oversimplified, because actually the *most* basic building
blocks of a language are the sounds from which the words are made. Oral

ings"), and they fall into different types or categories (called "parts of speech" or "word classes"). These words are combined into phrases, clauses, and sentences, and the sentences are in turn combined into paragraphs and sections. In this chapter, we will get started understanding these building blocks of communication by looking at the varied usages of words, at the different kinds of words ("parts of speech" or "word classes"), and at the way the words are related one to another (grammar or syntax).

Words and Their Usages

One of my mentors, Dr. Loyd Melton, is fond of beginning his New Testament interpretation classes in any given semester by placing a coffee cup on the table in front of him, pointing to it, and announcing, "That is a dog." He then proceeds to refer to the cup as a dog for the entire semester, and in imitation of him, the students often refer to their coffee cups as dogs when talking among themselves. Dr. Melton's point in this exercise is to show students that words do not have rigid meanings; they have **usages**. Another of my mentors, Dr. Matthew Ristuccia, expresses the same idea when he cautions his students, "Don't make a word into a term." Let us think about this idea for a moment.

The difference between a word and a term is that a word can be used in a variety of different ways in different situations and by different speakers/writers, whereas a **term** is a word that is always used the same way. Rarely is a word born as a term, since people do not normally make up a term by putting sounds together into a word no one has ever used before. More often, they take an existing word and make it into a term when they agree that they will use the word the same way every time. Terms are useful because they provide precision in communication, but

---

language is prior to and more foundational than written language, and by the time a language is written down, it has already passed its infancy and childhood and is into its adolescence. An important part of the study of language (even the study of a language one does not have to speak) is the study of its sound groups and how these combine to make roots, suffixes, and prefixes that shape the way the words will be used. In spite of the importance of this area of study, this book will not deal with it, but will instead take the words as the basic building blocks and focus on how those words are combined into phrases, clauses, and sentences.

until a group of people decides to make a word into a term, that word can be, and will be, used in various ways. Remember the word "get" from chapter 1. That word is used in many different ways in ordinary English. You would think nothing of using the word in two or three different ways in the same paragraph, or maybe even in the same sentence. For example, you might say, "When we all try to get into the car at the same time, I can't get over how big my children are getting." If you are talking to another native English speaker, it will be no problem at all for her to understand you, even though you have used the same word three different ways. Why does this not create a problem? Because English is our language. We instantly recognize any of the normal uses of the word "get," so even if one piles up three different usages of the word in one sentence, we can handle it without difficulty.

If, however, we use a word in a very different way from normal—for example, if we use the word "dog" to refer to a coffee cup or the word "corn" to refer to snow—then we will not communicate to most English speakers. Yet even here, if we are among Dr. Melton's students or are Colorado ski bums, then we can use these words in these unusual ways and still communicate perfectly, because the specific audience we are addressing is familiar with these usages of the words. To give you another example, one of my friends used to confuse words that had letters or sounds in common. He once wrote "wax" when he meant "wane," and he once said "repertoire" when he meant "rapport." I could understand him perfectly because I knew what he meant to say, and I also knew that I had to search my mind for words with sounds similar to the sounds in the word he actually said in order to find one that made sense in the context. I once told him, "You can use words any way you want when you are talking to me, and I'll still understand you, but if you want to communicate to anyone else, you need to use the words in more normal ways."

In the course of communication in a given language, the use of a given word might fall into three patterns. First, it would have one or more normal ways it is used, such as using "get" to mean "arrive at" or to mean "grow." This usage (or these usages) might be called the "definition" of the word or even the "meaning" of the word. In fact, however, this usage (or these usages) would actually be nothing more than the way (or ways) the word is used most of the time by most people. Second, a word might have some specialized or unusual usages among more limited audiences, like using "corn" to refer to snow or, in an even more limited case, using "dog" to refer to a coffee cup. Third, if a group of people like the medical community or the legal world actually decides to use a certain word the same way every time, and to teach students in that field to do likewise, then in that sphere the word becomes a term. When we are communicating in our own language, we have no difficulty recognizing the normal uses of a word, an unusual use of it, or a technical use of it as a term. The fact that a word can be used in many different ways, and even in three different patterns or categories of usages, is not a problem, because we effortlessly recognize and process these differences. We have been doing so our whole lives.

When one is working in another language, however, one is much less well equipped to handle this variety in word usage. A person's unconscious tendency is to assume that every word in that language must be used in one and only one way—it must have a single "meaning" or definition. One tends to forget that English does not work that way, and therefore one forgets that another language will not work that way, either. Because a beginning student unconsciously craves the simplicity of having each word of that language mean only one thing—or, to say it differently, having each word be a term—he subconsciously assumes that the language has to work that way. Of course, teachers and textbooks may unwittingly reinforce that mistaken idea when they give a single "definition" of each word. The language one is learning does not work that way, however, any more than English does. In any language, many words can be used in a range of different ways, and that range does not usually line up exactly with the way the corresponding words are used in another language. We saw some examples of this in chapter 1 (remember the *bleu* steak at the French restaurant); now let us take a look at a couple of examples from Greek and Latin.

As an illustration of the way different writers in the same language use the same word differently, consider the Greek word σάρξ [sarx], translated "flesh" in English. In the New Testament, Paul usually uses this word negatively, as a way of referring to the sinful tendency within each person. In Galatians 5:16–17, he writes: "Walk by the Spirit, and do not gratify the desires of the flesh. For the desires of the flesh are against the Spirit, and the desires of the Spirit are against the flesh." Here, σάρξ [sarx] or "flesh" is clearly used negatively, and in some Bible translations like the New International Version, the word is rendered "sinful nature" here, because the translators are trying to convey the fact that Paul is using the word negatively. In contrast, John uses the same word simply to refer to the body, the physical component of a person, without the pejorative connotation Paul attaches to the word. In John 1:14, he writes, "The Word became flesh and dwelt among us, full of grace and truth: we have beheld his glory, glory as of the only Son from the Father." Here there is no negative connotation to the word σάρξ [sarx], as there is in Galatians 5. The same Greek word is used in different ways, and some Bible translations, like the Revised Standard Version, expect the reader to recognize the different usages; others, like the New International Version, actually translate the word with different English words.

Now consider an example that involves both Greek and Latin. In the New Testament, the normal word for "worship" is προσκυνέω [proskyneō] (see Matthew 4:10, for example). The Latin word that is used to translate προσκυνέω [proskyneō] is adoro, but these two words do not line up closely with each other or with the English word "worship." The gist of the Greek word is "to bow," or "to prostrate oneself," and so the idea of worship in Greek is closely tied to the idea of submission to God. In Latin the idea of worship is closer to that of gazing in wonder at God's greatness (notice that we get our English word "adore" from this Latin word), and in English the root idea is that we ascribe worth to God; we declare him to be "worthy." The Greek, Latin, and English concepts of what worship involves are rather different, and so as one moves from Greek to Latin to English, the nuances of passages describing worship undergo some alteration.

Not only can a word be used in different ways in the same language, and not only do the uses of words not usually correspond perfectly from one language to another, but the normal use of a word can often change dramatically over time in the same language. As an English example, consider Paul's command in Philippians 4:6, rendered in the Revised Standard Version as, "Have no anxiety about anything." In the King James Version, this verse reads, "Be careful for nothing." Is one of these translations incorrect? No, the discrepancy comes about because the use of the word "careful" has changed in English between 1611 (when the King James was published) and the present. "Careful" comes from two words that combine to give the sense "full of care." We should recognize, however, that "full of care" can mean either "full of cares" (that is, "full of anxiety") or "full of precision." The Greek word μεριμνᾶτε [merimnate] used in this passage indicates the first of these, and that was the way the word "careful" was used in seventeenth-century English. Today, however, the word "careful" is almost always used to mean "full of precision," so another word, "anxious" (or the noun form "anxiety"), is needed in contemporary English to convey the idea of "careful" in seventeenth-century English.

Of course, what happens in English happens in other languages, as well. For example, the Greek word προσκυνέω [proskyneō], which we considered in the previous paragraph, was used to mean "bow before" or "to submit to" in the time of the New Testament. By the eighth century, that word had come to mean simply "to honor," and it became the word used to refer to the reverence that Christians give to saints, not the submission they give to God alone. (In the eighth century, the word for worship in the sense of submission to God was λατρεύω [latreuō].) A Greek word that had been used to mean "worship" or "submit" in the first century A.D. was not nearly as strong by the eighth century, so Christian writers needed to use a different word when describing worship.

Thus, we see that in any given language, words are used in ways that vary from author to author, from situation to situation, and from one time period to another. Most words are not terms, and it is a mistake to treat them as terms that can be used in only one way. Instead, beginning students of a foreign language need first to learn the basic or most common usages of each new vocabulary word. As they become more proficient (usually not before the second year of studying the language), students then need to study the ways key words are used in different situations, by different authors, and at different time periods. A great deal of the effort that advanced students put into a language goes toward understanding the contextual use of words in the literature they are studying. Such understanding will be crucial for a deep and accurate comprehension of that literature, because words and their various usages are the fundamental building block of communication in a given language.

For now, however, as you begin to study Greek or Latin, recognize that when you learn each new vocabulary word, what you are learning is not the one-and-only definition, but simply the most common way for that word to be used. You have to work from broad to narrow, from the way most writers of the language use the word to the way a more specific group or writer uses it.[2] As you gain more expertise, you may find yourself returning to that word later and learning other, more specialized ways it is used in certain contexts. If you recognize up front that this will happen, it will be easier for you later to make the transition from the most common use to the more specialized uses of the same word. To state this point another way, it will be easier for you to break out of the mentality that subconsciously turns all words into terms if you are reminded from day one that such a mentality is mistaken.

The Kinds of Words ("Parts of Speech" or "Word Classes")

It should be obvious by now that learning Greek or Latin involves understanding the different ways those languages relate words to one another. In order to begin this task, one must first understand the different categories into which one can place the various words of a language. These categories have long been called

2. When I give my students vocabulary quizzes, I do not ask them to *define* the words. Instead, I ask my students to give *a basic usage* for each word. My choice of words here serves as a reminder that what they are learning is not the only possible definition of a term, but one of the ways an everyday word can be used.

"parts of speech," although linguists today are more likely to call them "lexical categories" or "word classes." Whatever phrase one uses for them, these are the basic kinds of words one finds in a language, and in this book I will use the phrases "word classes," "categories of words," and "parts of speech" synonymously. The concept of parts of speech was devised by the Greeks, who argued about 100 B.C. that their language included eight categories of words: verbs, nouns, participles, articles, pronouns, adverbs, prepositions, and conjunctions. When the Romans later developed grammatical study of their own language, they felt compelled to retain the same number of categories the Greeks employed, but they had a problem in that Latin contained no articles (words equivalent to "the," "a," and "an" in English). So they added the category of interjections in order to retain the traditional number of word classes. Similarly, English grammar has typically been described in terms of the eight classes or parts of speech, but we normally add adjectives to the list in place of participles, and we consider articles to fall into the category of adjectives.

This brief history should show us that, to some degree, grammar is an artificial imposition on a language, and concerns such as preserving a perfect number like "eight" may lead one to subdivide a category that does not need dividing or to combine groups of words that might otherwise be in separate categories. Be that as it may, Greek, Latin, and English are all normally described in terms of eight parts of speech. As we continue looking at the building blocks of language in this chapter, let us consider these word classes, all of which you will become thoroughly familiar with as you study Greek or Latin. As I describe these kinds of words, I will illustrate them with examples from English.

Nouns. These are words that name persons ("Peter"), places ("Rome"), things ("book"), or ideas/virtues/qualities ("wisdom"). They can also name groups of persons, places, or things. For example, "Peter" is the name of a particular person, whereas "crowd" is the name of a certain group of people. "Tool" is the name of a broad group or class of things, of which "scalpel" is a specific example. Greek, Latin, and English grammarians have all considered nouns to be a part of speech.

Adjectives. These are words that describe a person (*"bold* Peter"), place (*"glorious* Rome"), thing (*"sharp* scalpel"), or idea (*"abundant* wisdom"). Because adjectives describe the qualities of someone or something, they are sometimes said to qualify the word they go with. Or, sometimes they are said to modify the word, in that they alter its meaning by making it more specific. Hence, adjectives are often called **qualifiers** or **modifiers**. Greek and Latin grammarians did not consider adjectives to be a part of speech. This was because adjectives were formed the same way as nouns (as we shall see later in this book), and thus they could be classified grammatically in the same category as nouns. Most textbooks of Greek and Latin today follow the English practice of considering adjectives a word class.

Articles (sometimes called "determiners"). These are words that specify definitely or indefinitely which particular person, place, thing, or idea one is referring to. The **definite article** in English is "the," as in the example, "the book that is on the table." The **indefinite article** in English is "a" or "an," as in the example, "a book about Greek." The first of these examples is referring to a specific book and is identifying it definitely: *the* book that is on the table (and evidently there is only one book on the table right now). The second example is not referring to a specific book, but to any book about a particular subject, so it uses the indefinite article. English thus has both an indefinite article and a definite article. Greek has a definite article—an equivalent to the word "the"—but not an indefinite article. Latin has neither an indefinite nor a definite article. In chapter 5, we will look at the implications of the presence or absence of an article for the way these languages express the same idea. Obviously, Latin grammarians could not consider articles to be a part of speech, since their language had none. The Greeks did consider articles a part of speech. Some English grammarians do as well, although more commonly, English grammarians consider articles to be a subcategory of adjectives.[3]

3. Some grammarians consider articles to be a subcategory of pronouns, since they began historically as pronouns. To me, however, it makes more sense to consider them as adjectives. Regardless of how they began, they are

Pronouns. These are words that take the place of nouns. They refer to a particular person, place, thing, or idea without forcing the speaker or writer to name it again. For example, consider the following: "The book that is on the table is very good. I enjoyed reading it." Here, both "that" and "it" are pronouns, and both of them refer to the book. These pronouns enable one to refer to the book multiple times without having to repeat the word in a cumbersome way. To see the elegance that pronouns add to a language, consider how much clumsier it would be to say the following: "The book is on the table. The book is very good. I enjoyed reading the book." Greek, Latin, and English grammarians have all considered pronouns to be a word class.

Verbs. These are words that describe an action or a state of being. For example, when we say "the book *is* on the table," we are describing a state, but when we say, "I *read* the book," we are describing an action. In both cases, the central "event" of the sentence—whether action or state—is expressed by the verb. We saw in chapter 1 that in English, a verb is so essential to a sentence that there can be no complete sentence without one, but in Greek and Latin, an idea—especially a state—can be expressed without a verb. This is because in those languages, one may assume a certain state even if no verb is present. One can say, "the book—good," and the reader will understand the state well enough that no verb is necessary. Greek, Latin, and English grammarians have all considered verbs to be a part of speech.

Participles. These are verbal forms that function in some other way—usually like adjectives. Thus, participles can be considered as a part of speech in their own right or can be treated grammatically in connection with verbs—the words from which they come—or in connection with the words they replace—adjectives and nouns. In ancient times, the Greeks and Latins considered participles to be a word class. English grammarians usually do not. Most Greek and Latin grammar books written in English consider participles under the category of verbs.

---

not pronouns any longer, because they are used with nouns rather than in place of nouns.

Adverbs. These are words that express some quality related to a verb or an attribute. For example, in the sentence "Hudson runs very quickly," the verb is "runs," and both "very" and "quickly" are adverbs that qualify how he runs. "Quickly" modifies the verb "runs," and "very" modifies the adverb "quickly." (Consider that one could have said, "Hudson runs somewhat quickly" or "Hudson runs rather quickly," and in either case the meaning would have been different from "Hudson runs very quickly.") Thus, adverbs can modify a verb or another adverb that is itself modifying a verb. Similarly, an adverb can modify an adjective, as in the sentence "Hudson is very quick." In this instance, "very" modifies "quick," but "quick" is an adjective, not an adverb, because it modifies "Hudson" and describes something about him as a person (not something about what he is doing right now, as in "Hudson runs very quickly.") Greek, Latin, and English grammarians have all considered adverbs to be a part of speech.

Prepositions. These are words that show the relation between a noun or pronoun and some other word in the sentence. In the sentence, "the book *on* the table is red," the relation between two nouns—the book and the table—is expressed by the preposition "on." In the sentence "Randy ran *into* the room," the preposition "into" expresses the relation between a noun—"the room"—and an action—Randy's running. The noun or pronoun to which the preposition pertains is called the **object of the preposition**. The group of words that includes the preposition, its object, and any words that modify the object is called a **prepositional phrase**. A prepositional phrase can be used to modify a noun (as in the example "the book *on the table* is red"), in which case it functions as an adjective, so one can say that the phrase is used adjectivally. Or a prepositional phrase can be used to modify a verb (as in the example "Randy ran *into the room*"), in which case it is used adverbially. Greek, Latin, and English grammarians have all considered prepositions to be a word class.

Conjunctions. These are words that link or connect words or groups of words without altering their grammatical relations. Consider the following examples, all of which use the conjunction "and": "Aaron *and* Melanie study Latin together." "To do well in Greek, you need to devote adequate time to study *and* to use that time well." "The teacher knows Latin well, *and* the students are making progress in the language every day." In the first case, the conjunction "and" links two words; in the second case it links two phrases (a word I will define a bit later in this section), and in the third case the conjunction links two clauses (a word I will also define later). There are two kinds of conjunctions: **coordinate conjunctions**, which link equivalent elements, and **subordinate conjunctions**, which introduce a subordinate clause and thus link it to a main clause. Greek, Latin, and English grammarians have all considered conjunctions to be a part of speech.

Interjections. These are words that are simply inserted into speech or writing as exclamations, and that thus have little grammatical connection to the words around them. In many cases, these words offer a way to express surprise, anger, or some other emotion in a very simple way, without altering the grammar of the sentences around them. Colloquial speech is full of interjections, but at least in English, they are not as common in formal writing. For example, in the sentence "*Oh,* I wish I could go with you," the word "oh" is an interjection, and it is essentially unrelated to the rest of the sentence. Interjections constitute a good example of the somewhat arbitrary nature of grammatical classification. Many interjections started out as adverbs, as adjectives (as "oh" in the example above), or even as nouns (as would be the case in the example "*Man,* I wish I could go with you," in which "man" is obviously a noun, but here it is not used to refer to a particular man whom the speaker is addressing; it has become a simple interjection). Thus, one could classify them as the part of speech in which they began, and this is what Greek grammarians in the ancient world did. Today, since grammarians are following Latin, they usually consider interjections to be a class of words.

From these descriptions, one should notice again that Greek, Latin, and English grammarians have not always classified their words the same way. Table 3-1 (page 38) summarizes the slight variations in classification.

These slight differences should not blind us to the fact that in the case of these three languages, there is substantial overlap

Table 3-1 Word Classes in Greek, Latin, and English

Greek	Latin	English
1. Nouns	1. Nouns	1. Nouns
		2. Adjectives
2. Articles		[Articles]
3. Pronouns	2. Pronouns	3. Pronouns
4. Verbs	3. Verbs	4. Verbs
5. Participles	4. Participles	
6. Adverbs	5. Adverbs	5. Adverbs
7. Prepositions	6. Prepositions	6. Prepositions
8. Conjunctions	7. Conjunctions	7. Conjunctions
	8. Interjections	8. Interjections

in the word classes. In fact, there is so much overlap that describing Greek and Latin in terms of the eight categories English grammarians normally use is convenient and perfectly acceptable, even though these are not exactly the eight categories the ancient Greeks and Romans used themselves. This is what most Greek and Latin textbooks written in English do.

In addition to these parts of speech or word classes, there are two other widely used terms you will need to know, and both of these terms apply to groups of word classes. The first term is **particle**, which refers to any part of speech (word class) whose words, in Greek and Latin, do not change their form. In those two languages, nouns, adjectives (including articles), pronouns, and especially verbs change their form depending on how they relate to the words around them. English words in three of these four word classes do the same thing, but to a much lesser degree. For example, "book" can become "books"; "he" can become "him"; and "run" can become "runs." Adjectives do not change their form in English (whether one is speaking of one book or many, the adjective "good" would not change: compare "one good book" to "many good books"), but they do in Greek and Latin. The other four classes—adverbs, prepositions, conjunctions, and interjections—consist of words that never change their form, even in Greek and Latin; these classes collectively are called particles.

The other term you will need to know is **substantive**, which refers to any word that can refer to a person, place, thing, or idea. (You can remember the term more easily if you think of it as referring to a "substance" of some kind.) In other words, a substantive is a noun or any word or combination of words that can take the place of a noun. Pronouns are obviously substantives, and in English certain verbal forms can also be substantives. For example, in the sentences "*Swimming* is fun" and "It is fun *to swim*," the italicized portions are actually used as nouns (they describe the thing the sentence is about), but the words themselves come from the verb "swim." In Latin there are more word classes that can be used as substantives than there are in English, and in Greek, virtually any word in the language can be used as a substantive under certain circumstances. So the variety of ways one can create a substantive in these two languages is a major difference between both of them on one hand, and English on the other. When one uses a word besides a noun or a pronoun as a substantive, this is called a "substantive use" of that word, or using the word "substantively."

The Ways Words Are Related to One Another

I wrote earlier in this chapter that words are the building blocks of language communication. This is true, but it is an oversimplification, because it is not individual words that communicate, but rather words as they are arranged into groups.[4] In any language, speakers and writers convey meaning not just by

---

4. I once had a Ukrainian friend who knew a large number of English words, but almost no English grammar. Whenever he would try to speak to me in English, I could not make any sense of the jumble of apparently unrelated words that came out of his mouth. Only if I could get him to say the sentence in Russian, and thus to give me a structure for understanding the English words, could I put the English words he was saying together into a sentence that made sense. Because he did not know the English way to relate the words one to another, he could not communicate effectively in English.

the ways they use words, or even by the kinds of words (word classes or parts of speech) they use, but by the ways they relate the words to one another. As a result, grammar is divided into two broad categories, one of which has to do with the forms the words take (this is called **morphology** or **accidence**), and the other of which has to do with how the words are related to one another (called **syntax**). Morphology comes from the Greek word for "form," and the question of how one makes a certain adjective as opposed to an adverb (remember "quick" and "quickly" in English) or how one indicates that a verb pertains to the past rather than the future ("he ran" vs. "he will run" in English) is a question of morphology. Similarly, "accidence" comes from the Latin word for the incidental parts of words, the parts that can change without affecting the basic idea the word conveys. A great deal of the memory work you will have to do in Greek or Latin will pertain to morphology or accidence; you will need to memorize the forms that various words can take in different situations. Morphology is important in most languages, but it is especially important in Greek and Latin, for reasons I will explain later in this section.

On the other hand, "syntax" comes from the Greek verb meaning "to arrange" and concerns the way words and groups of words are ordered within a sentence so as to make their relations clear. These groups of words fall into two main categories: **phrases** and **clauses**. A phrase is a group of words that functions as a unit, and the phrase is usually dominated by a central word that determines what kind of group the phrase is. One can have a **noun phrase**, in which the dominant word is a noun and is surrounded by modifiers. One can also have a **verb phrase**, an **adjective phrase**, an **adverb phrase**, or a **prepositional phrase** (which we have already encountered). Consider the following example: "Give the book to the not-so-tall girl talking too noisily over there." This sentence is not particularly good English style, but it is comprehensible, and it contains several different kinds of phrases. First, it contains a prepositional phrase, consisting of the preposition ("to"), the object of the preposition ("girl"), and all modifiers ("the not-so-tall" and "talking too noisily over there"). Furthermore, this prepositional phrase has several phrases within it. All the words except for the preposition itself (that is, "the not-so-tall girl talking too noisily over there") constitute a noun phrase, of which the controlling word is the noun "girl." The words "the not-so-tall" comprise an adjective phrase. The words "talking too noisily over there" comprise a verb phrase. Within the verb phrase, the words "too noisily" constitute an adverb phrase. In each case, a group of words comprises a unit, and the unit performs the function of a single noun, verb, adjective, or adverb. Consider that one could say the following: "Give the book to the tall girl talking noisily over there." In this case, "noisily" is simply an adverb, but in the other case, "too noisily" does the work of an adverb, but since it includes two words, it is an adverb phrase. Similarly, "tall" in the second case is simply an adjective, but "not-so-tall" in the first case is an adjective phrase, because a group of words does the function of a single part of speech. A great deal of your study of syntax will involve learning to recognize which words go together to make certain phrases, and how those phrases fit together. For now, the main point to recognize is that if a particular kind of word (an adverb, a noun) can function in a certain way in a sentence, then a group of words (an adverb phrase or a noun phrase) can function in the same way. One can use a group of words to perform the function that a single word would normally perform.

In contrast to phrases, **clauses** are groups of words that include a **subject** and a **predicate** and that thus express a complete idea. Remember from chapter 1 that a subject is the person, place, thing, or idea about which one is speaking, and a predicate is what one is saying about that person, place, or thing. Remember also that in English, a predicate must include a verb, but in many languages (including Greek and Latin), one may have a predicate without a verb. Furthermore, in Greek and Latin, the subject may often be implied rather than expressed. The verb forms of these two languages imply a certain subject, so instead of writing "he," "she," "we," in front of the verb, one can indicate the subject by the ending on the verb. In Latin, *amamus* means "we love," and if it is clear who "we" are, then the subject does not need to be expressed. So *amamus* by itself can be considered a clause or even a sentence, because it has an implied subject "we" and it includes a predicate, an action. Thus, the distinction between a phrase and a clause, which is rather clear-cut in English, is a bit murkier in Greek and Latin. In fact, in those languages, one defines a clause in terms of the presence of a particular kind of verb form, called a finite verb, and we will not be able to consider what constitutes a clause in Greek or Latin until we have probed verbs a bit more thoroughly. For now, the point is that Latin and especially Greek often use phrases where English has to use clauses, and so the distinction between a phrase and a clause is not as crucial for understanding those languages as it is for understanding English.

Consider again the earlier example: "Give the book to the girl talking over there." In this sentence, the word "talking" is a verb form, and the verb phrase "talking over there" modifies "girl." Another way to say this would be the following: "Give the book to the girl who is talking over there." In this case, "who is talking over there" is now a clause because there is an expressed subject, "who." This is a **subordinate clause**, because it could not form a sentence in its own right. (One could not say simply, "Who is talking over there" by itself.) A subordinate clause depends on another clause and functions dependently in the sentence. A clause that can stand on its own (that *could* be a complete sentence, even if it is not) is called an **independent clause**. In this example, "Give the book to the girl" is an independent clause. So in English the distinction between the phrase and the clause is fairly clear-cut, and in most cases, English would prefer to use the clause rather than the phrase. In Greek and Latin, stating this idea with a phrase would be far more common than using a clause.

If sentences are composed of words that are grouped into phrases and clauses, how does a given language indicate the relations between these words, phrases, and clauses? In English, the relations between the words and phrases are indicated in two primary ways. First, and most important, the order of the words indicates how they are related to one another. Consider the following example, in the context of a wedding ceremony: "David gives Tom Mary." If you know the context, you will be able to recognize that David is the bride's father, Mary is the bride, and Tom is the groom. The bride's father is symbolically giving the bride to the groom to be married. In such a sentence, the first noun ("David") must be the subject (the one doing the giving), the noun at the end ("Mary") must be the object (the one being given), and the person to whom the object is given must be named immediately before the object. Without this rigid word order, a sentence such as this would break down and be incomprehensible.

Second, in English one also conveys the relations between the words and phrases by adding other words that indicate such relations. For example, in a prepositional phrase, the preposition itself is added to convey a particular kind of relation between the object and the rest of the sentence. One could restate the previous example like this: "David gives Mary to Tom." In this case, the preposition "to" indicates that Tom is in a certain relation to David and Mary, and so the word "to" serves the same function as the placement of the word "Tom" indicated in the previous sentence. Likewise, linking two phrases or clauses with "and" relates them to each other in a very different way than linking them with "but." One could say, "Tom proposed to Mary, and she accepted him," or one could say, "Tom proposed to Mary, but she accepted him." In the first case, it is clear that Mary was expected to accept Tom's proposal, but in the second, it is clear that she was expected to reject it. The fact that she accepted him in the second case comes as a surprise. Thus, the use of prepositions, conjunctions, and other words establishes certain kinds of relations between words, phrases, and clauses.

This is precisely where Greek and Latin begin to diverge most radically from English. The classical languages do not primarily rely on word order or the addition of "marker" words to show the relation between words, phrases, and clauses. There are cases where the words must be put in a certain order, but far more often, the word order is variable. While Greek and Latin do have a number of conjunctions and prepositions, they have far fewer than English has and do not need them nearly as often. This is because Greek and Latin convey the relations between words primarily by the forms of those words. Consider again the example "David gave Mary to Tom." In Greek or Latin, the form of the word "David" would indicate that he is the subject of the sentence (the one doing the action), so that word could go anywhere in the sentence with no ambiguity. Similarly, the form of "Tom" would indicate that he is the one receiving the action, and the form of "Mary" would indicate that she is the one being given. Because these forms convey the relations between the words, the author is free to write the words in any order. Also, since the form of "Tom" would imply that he is receiving the action, there would be no need for a preposition like "to."

The changes in the form of a word as that word assumes different functions in a sentence are called **inflection**. In English, most words have no inflection (that is, they never change, regardless of where they occur in a sentence or how they are used). Only nouns, pronouns, and verbs are inflected, and even these parts of speech undergo only minor changes. We have seen that nouns change from singular to plural ("book" vs. "books"), and they also have possessive forms ("book's," as in the sentence, "The book's title is rather strange.") Pronouns exhibit a bit more variety—"I," "me," "mine," "we," "us," "ours." Verbs likewise have a bit of variety—"drop," "drops," "dropped," "dropping"— but these changes in the forms of words are quite minor. For the most part, English relies on word order and helping words to convey the relations between words. Languages in which the words do not change form very much are called **analytic languages**. In contrast, languages in which the forms of the words change dramatically (that is, highly inflected languages, since "inflection" refers to the changes in the word forms) are called **synthetic languages**. Greek and Latin are highly synthetic languages, whereas English is a highly analytic language.[5]

This difference, more than anything else, is what creates

---

5. Some Asian tongues, such as Chinese and Vietnamese, are the most analytic of all modern languages in the world. Among modern European languages, English is the most analytic, followed by the Romance languages (French, Spanish, Portuguese, Italian, and Romanian). The Slavic languages (Russian, Byelorussian, Ukrainian, Polish, Bulgarian, Serbian, and Croatian), as well as Finnish and Hungarian, are the most synthetic modern

problems for English-speaking students of Greek and Latin. Accordingly, this is the point at which you, as a new student, need to recognize what lies ahead of you. As I have already hinted, the number of forms you will have to memorize will be daunting, and it will be especially daunting if you do not recognize why all those forms are necessary. The longer you remain in English mode, the more frustrated you are likely to become with the fact that Greek and Latin nouns, adjectives, and especially verbs can take so many different forms. You may want to say in exasperation, "Why do they need a different form to tell me that the word 'run' is in the future? Why can't they just put the word 'will' in front of it like we do, to make 'will run'?" If you take that kind of attitude into the study of Greek or Latin, you are in for a long, frustrating period of study. In contrast, if you go into the study of the language recognizing that it is just as reasonable to change the form of a verb as it is to add another word to make the verb refer to the future, you will likely find Latin or Greek to be less daunting and more enjoyable. Similarly, if you recognize up front that changing the form of a noun is just as good a way to indicate its relation to other nouns as putting it in a certain place in the sentence or adding a certain preposition in front of it, then you are much more likely to enjoy Greek or Latin. In fact, you may find that there are many advantages to a highly inflected (that is, synthetic) language. Foremost among them is the fact that if you can use forms to convey relations between words, you can use word order to do something else, like emphasize particular words more strongly than others. A synthetic language like Greek or Latin holds out many possibilities for communicating emphasis and nuance that are harder for an analytic language like English to accomplish. You may find, as I do, that you actually prefer synthetic languages like Greek or Latin; even if you do not, you may at least be able to appreciate those languages.

European languages. German is moderately synthetic, although it also depends heavily on word order.

In this chapter I have sought to focus on three aspects of language that beginning students need to recognize and study. The first is the fact that words can be used in a variety of ways, and that study of a language involves learning the general patterns of usage early on, and then later the specific usage in the literature one is reading. The second is the fact that there are different kinds of words (parts of speech or word classes), and while the categories for describing these kinds of words are somewhat arbitrary, we must have some sort of categorization scheme in order to talk about how words relate to one another, and thus, in order to understand how languages work. The third is the fact that Latin and Greek convey the relations between words, phrases, and clauses in ways very different from the way English does. In the remainder of this book, I will seek to build on the grammatical savvy you are developing by looking in more detail at the way the various classes of Latin and Greek words inflect (that is, how they change their form) and function (that is, how they are related to other words). I will begin with nouns, adjectives, articles (although not everyone considers articles to be a separate word class from adjectives), and pronouns, which will be the subject of part 2.

APPENDIX: GRAMMATICAL TERMS INTRODUCED IN CHAPTER 3

Accidence: The changes that the forms of words undergo as they serve different functions in a sentence. See also **Inflection, Morphology.**

Adjective: A word that describes a person (*"bold* Peter"), place (*"glorious* Rome"), thing (*"sharp* scalpel"), or idea (*"abundant* wisdom"). An adjective is said to modify or qualify the meaning of the word it goes with, so it is a kind of modifier or qualifier.

Adjective phrase: A group of words that, taken together, function as an adjective.

Adverb: A word that expresses some quality related to a verb or an attribute. An adverb can modify a verb ("he runs *quickly*"), an adjective ("he is *very* quick"), or another adverb ("he runs *very* quickly"). An adverb is a kind of modifier or qualifier.

Adverb phrase: A group of words that, taken together, function as an adverb.

Analytic language: A language in which there are relatively few changes in the forms of words, and thus in which word order is the primary way of showing the relations between words. English is a highly analytic language.

Article: A word that specifies definitely (*"the* book") or indefinitely (*"a* book") which particular person, place, thing, or idea one is referring to. An article is also called a "determiner."

Clause: In Greek or Latin, a group of words that includes a subject and a predicate, and in which the predicate is expressed by a finite verb form.

Conjunction: A word that links or connects words or groups of words without altering their grammatical relations (e.g., *and, but, because, since*).

Coordinate conjunction: A conjunction that links grammatically equivalent words or groups of words (e.g., "David *and* Mary are here").

Definite article: An article that identifies a particular person, place, thing, or idea specifically, so as to distinguish it from other similar people, places, things, or ideas (e.g., *"the* book that is on the table"). Greek has a definite article, but Latin does not.

Independent clause: A clause that expresses a complete idea and stands on its own as a sentence, or that could stand on its own, even if it is part of a longer sentence.

Indefinite article: An article that identifies a person, place, thing, or idea in a non-specific way (e.g., *"a* book about Rome"). Greek and Latin have no indefinite article.

Inflection: The changes in the form of a word as that word assumes different functions in a sentence. See also **Accidence**, **Morphology**.

Interjection: A word that is inserted into speech or writing as an exclamation, and that thus has little grammatical connection to the words around it (e.g., *"oh,* that was a good movie").

Modifier: A word that alters the meaning of the word it goes with, usually by making it more specific.

Morphology: The study of the forms words take in a given language in order to fulfill the functions those words play in a sentence. See also **Accidence, Inflection.**

Noun: A word that names a person (*Peter*), a place (*Rome*), a thing (*book*), or an idea/virtue/quality (*wisdom*). A noun can also name a group of persons, places, things, or ideas.

Noun phrase: A group of words that, taken together, function as a noun.

Object of preposition: The noun or pronoun to which a preposition pertains (e.g., "the book on the *table* is red"). In Greek the object always comes after the preposition, and in Latin it normally comes after.

Part of speech: A term for the basic category to which a word belongs. Grammarians often divide Greek or Latin words into eight parts of speech. See also **Word class.**

Participle: A verbal form that functions in some other way, usually as an adjective (e.g., "the girl *standing* over there").

Phrase: A group of words that, taken together, function as unit.

Preposition: A word that shows the relation between a noun or pronoun and some other word in the sentence (e.g., "the book *on* the table is red").

Prepositional phrase: A group of words that includes a preposition, its object, and any words that modify the object (e.g., "the book *on the table* is red").

Pronoun: A word that takes the place of a noun. It refers to a particular person, place, thing, or idea without forcing the speaker or writer to name it again (e.g., "Here is the book I was talking about. Have you read *it*?").

Qualifier: A word that describes the qualities of the word it goes with. See also **Adjective.**

Subordinate clause: A clause that depends on another clause and thus cannot form a sentence in its own right (e.g., "the boy *who is talking over there* is tall").

Subordinate conjunction: A conjunction that links a subordinate clause to a main clause (e.g., "*because* you are learning Latin, you have to study hard").

Syntax: The study of the way words and groups of words are ordered within a sentence so as to make their relations clear.

Synthetic language: A language in which changes in the forms of words (**inflection**) are the primary means of showing the relations between the words. Greek and Latin are highly synthetic languages.

Term: A word that is always used the same way by a particular group of people.

Usage of words: The patterns according to which speakers/writers of a given language convey meaning through words. There are three basic patterns of word usage. The first involves the most common usages of a given word, ones that any native speaker of the language would recognize. The second involves the more specialized or unusual usages of a word among more limited audiences. The third pattern involves a group of people deciding in an official fashion to use a certain word the same way every time, and to teach students in that field to do likewise; in that sphere the word becomes a **term**.

Verb: A word that describes the "event" of the sentence, usually an action ("I *read* the book") or a state of being ("the book *is* on the table").

Verb phrase: A group of words that, taken together, function as a verb.

Word class: Another term for **part of speech**, which refers to the basic category to which a word belongs.

PART 2 **NOUNS AND THE WORDS THAT GO WITH THEM**

4

EXPRESSING THE RELATIONS
BETWEEN NOUNS

The previous chapter introduced the distinction between analytic and synthetic languages—that is, between languages that use word order and helping words to show how the main words are related, and languages that use changes in the forms of the words to convey those relations. English is a highly analytic language; it relies more heavily on word order and less on inflection (differences in forms) than any other modern European language. As we begin trying to grasp how an inflected language like Greek or Latin shows the relations between words, we need to introduce the idea of **cases**, and I will describe cases in this chapter through a three-step process. First, I will use what limited examples there are in English to show that you already have some basic familiarity with cases, even if you do not recognize this fact yet. Second, I will explain how cases grow out of eight basic *functions* in Indo-European languages in general. (I will explain the phrase "Indo-European" as part of that discussion.) Third, I will introduce you to the specifics of the case system in Greek and Latin. Once I have introduced the case system by these steps, I will close the chapter by briefly discussing the noun forms you will have to learn as you study Greek or Latin.

Cases—Not a Completely Foreign Idea

Remember the example from the previous chapter connected with a wedding: "David gives Tom Mary" or "David gives Mary to Tom." Let us use the second way of expressing this idea, since that way is more natural English, and let us substitute pronouns for the nouns. (Remember that a pronoun is a word that takes the place of a noun.) In this case, we have, "He gives her to him." Notice the difference between the word "he" and the word "him." The function of each of these words is not demonstrated *merely* by its place in the sentence's word order, although one would still want to put the words in the same order in most cases. In addition, the *form* of the word indicates its function. "He" is used to indicate the person who is doing the action, or the "subject." The form "him" is used to indicate the person receiving the action, or the "object." In this case, the word "him" is the object of the preposition "to," thus indicating to whom Mary is being given. Now consider a different example from the same wedding: "The veil Mary is wearing is Cindy's." Once again, let us change the nouns to pronouns. We now have, "The veil she is wearing is hers." In this case, the forms "Cindy's" and "hers" are possessives; they indicate that the veil belongs to Cindy, even though Mary is wearing it (although notice that with pronouns, that sentence is ambiguous about which woman the veil belongs to), whereas the forms "Mary" and "she" indicate that Mary is the subject of the action—she is the one wearing the veil. From these examples, we see that English pronouns change form to indicate different ways of relating words. Whether Tom is the one doing the action or receiving the action, the noun "Tom" keeps the same form, but the different words "he" and "him" indicate that there are different forms for the one doing or receiving the action.

These differences in form to reflect different functions are called **cases**. In English, there are three cases, but most of the time we see the changes in form only with pronouns, not actually with nouns. We are not worried about English grammar here, but just so we will have some labels for the following discussion, I will give you the names of the three English cases: nominative ("he" or "she"), objective ("him" or "her"), and possessive ("his" or "hers"). The nominative case is for "naming" the person, place, thing, or idea that is the subject, the one doing the action of a sentence. The objective case is for the "object," that is, for the one receiving the action of a verb or a preposition. The pos-

Table 4-1 First-Person Pronouns in English

	Singular	Plural
Nominative Case	I	we
Possessive Case	mine	ours
Objective Case	me	us

sessive case is for the one who/that possesses something else or someone else. Nouns themselves use the same form for the nominative and the objective, but have a different form for the possessive case. Pronouns usually have different forms for the three cases. In addition, nouns and pronouns have different forms for singular and for plural—"book" vs. "books." The change from singular to plural is called number, so grammatically, if one asks what "number" a form is, the answer (in English—not in all languages) is either "singular" or "plural." Thus, in English, when one combines the three cases with the two numbers, there are six possible forms for a noun or pronoun (although again, only pronouns actually exhibit all of these different forms). Tables 4-1 to 4-3 illustrate these possibilities.

Table 4-1 is for the pronoun "I," which we call the **first-person pronoun** because it refers to the person who is speaking or writing the sentence. Notice that there are different forms for all six possibilities.

Table 4-2 (page 56) is for the pronoun "you," which we call the **second-person pronoun** because it refers to the person who is being addressed in the sentence. Notice that *today* there is no difference between singular and plural forms in formal English. In colloquial English, the plural of "you" becomes "you guys" or "y'all," but in formal English it is still "you." As table 4-2 also shows, there used to be a distinction in number: "thou" and its various forms were for singular; "ye" and its various forms were for plural. We see vestiges of this today when people pray using archaic English, but most of the time there is no distinction. English has lost a bit of the complexity it used to have, and as a

Table 4-2   Second-Person Pronouns in English

	Singular	Plural
Nominative Case	you [thou]	you [ye]
Possessive Case	yours [thine]	yours
Objective Case	you [thee]	you

Table 4-3   Third-Person Pronouns in English

	Singular	Plural
Nominative Case	he, she, it	they
Possessive Case	his, hers, its	theirs
Objective Case	him, her, it	them

result, in a modern Bible translation, one cannot tell whether "you" is meant to be singular or plural. In the King James Version (or for that matter, in a translation of the Bible into almost any other language), one would be able to tell the difference.

Table 4-3 is for "he," "she," and "it," and we call this the **third-person pronoun** because it refers to a third party, to someone besides the speaker or the person being addressed. Notice that the forms are distinct, as in the case of the first-person pronoun, but in contrast to the second-person pronoun.

There are two reasons for showing you these tables and discussing these English cases. First, and most important, I do this to help you recognize that you are already familiar with the idea of using different cases for different functions. You have been doing this in English your whole life, albeit only to a limited degree. Therefore, as we turn to the cases of Greek and Latin, you should not feel as if you are entering a different world altogether.

Second, I show you these pronouns to help you recognize that English is not static; it is constantly changing and evolving. Four hundred years ago, when the King James Version of the Bible was translated, English had more pronouns in common use than it does today. A thousand years ago, English had different forms for its nouns and pronouns, but it lost its different case forms for nouns early in its literary history, and more recently it has been losing some of the pronoun case forms (the separate forms for "you" singular and "you" plural), as well. English is becoming less synthetic and thus more analytic as it goes along. This is part of the reason people have so much trouble remembering whether "I" or "me" is correct. The function of the pronoun, we subconsciously think, is determined by its place in the sentence, not by its form. So we often get the forms wrong. As we saw in the introduction, we say, "Me and Paul are going to lunch." In this sentence, the pronoun should be "I" because it is referring to one of the people doing the action, but the position of the pronoun at the beginning of the sentence is in and of itself sufficient to show that it refers to the doer of the action. Because of this, there is no confusion or ambiguity about this sentence. It is not correct, but it communicates perfectly clearly, because in an analytic language like English, the location of a word is more important than its form. Similarly, we saw that "just between you and I" is incorrect, but even so, it is perfectly clear. The placement of the word "I" is sufficient to indicate that it is one of the objects of the preposition "between," so even when we use the wrong form, we still communicate well. English is becoming more analytic all the time, and one of the symptoms of this trend is the fact that ordinary English speakers have trouble inflecting the forms of their own language correctly.

Even though English functions well while losing its few remaining inflected forms, consider for a moment the value of having such forms. Take this sentence: "They did not see him." Now suppose you want to say this, but you want to emphasize *him*. You can change the order of the words to "Him they did not see." This is still good English, because the word "him" is in the objective case and the word "they" is in the nominative case. Thus, there is no ambiguity about which word refers to the ones who do the action and which word refers to the one who receives it. In the case of pronouns, when we have both inflection and word order at our disposal, we can use inflection to convey the relations between the words and word order for emphasis. So we have flexibility for expressing and emphasizing ideas. Notice, however, what happens when we change from pronouns to nouns: "The people did not see Jesus." In this case we cannot reverse the order without doing damage to the sentence: "Jesus did not see the people" would mean something different, and "Jesus the people did not see" would be ambiguous. (It could mean either that Jesus did not see the people or that the people did not see Jesus.) If we were working in a language that inflects its nouns as well as its pronouns, then we could change the order of this second sentence, thus adding the emphasis where we want to put it without creating confusion or ambiguity. Having distinct forms for different cases can be very useful for people communicating in a given language, although admittedly it is harder for a student to learn these additional forms.

Cases in Indo-European Languages—Indicators of *Function*

In English, as we have seen, there are only three cases, and so one has to use word order and prepositions to convey most relations between nouns or pronouns and other words in the sentence. In some languages there are many more cases, so one can convey more of the basic relations between words by case forms without resorting to word order or adding prepositions. In spite of the variety in the number of cases from one language to another, the cases in most of the European languages have some basic similarities, because these languages belong to the same language family. This is called the Indo-European (or sometimes "Indo-Germanic") family because languages of this type became common both in India and on the European continent in antiquity. The ancient languages Latin, Greek, and Sanskrit (a language of early India) are themselves descendants of an originally common Indo-European language, usually referred to as the "parent" of those languages and sometimes called "proto-Indo-European." Modern European languages such as Greek, English, French,

Spanish, Portuguese, Italian, Romanian, German, Dutch, Swedish, Norwegian, Russian, Ukrainian, Polish, Serbian, Croatian, and Bulgarian all belong to this family, as well.[1]

In the Indo-European languages, there are eight basic kinds of relations between nouns, probably corresponding to eight different cases in the parent language.[2] At this point I would like to discuss these eight cases and how they are used to relate words to one another. Accordingly, you need to remember that for now we are discussing function, not form. Differences in function do not always correspond to differences in form, and I will discuss the forms of the Greek and Latin cases in the next section of this chapter. Most beginning textbooks of the classical languages start from form (you learn the forms for the different cases) and then work their way to function (you learn several different ways each case can be used). I believe it is more helpful to start with function in general, then proceed to the forms (the actual cases and what they look like), and then look at function in more detail (the specific uses of each case). Therefore, as I introduce the Indo-European cases here, I will use the word "function" to remind you that I am talking about how words are used and related to one another, not yet about what form those words take.

Nominative Function. The word "nominative" comes from the Latin for "to name," and it thus conveys the idea of naming a person, place, thing, or idea. The nominative function is the task of expressing the subject about whom/which one is speaking or writing in the sentence. In English, as we know, the nominative function is usually performed by placing a certain word first (or at least early) in the sentence, although we also know that pronouns have a specific form to indicate that those words perform the nominative function. In the sentence, "Not seeing what lay

---

1. The major modern European languages that are not Indo-European are Finnish, Estonian, and Hungarian, which belong to the Finno-Ugric family. In the Middle East, Hebrew, Aramaic, Syriac, and Arabic belong to the Semitic family and work very differently from the Indo-European languages.

2. I write "probably" because we do not have written evidence of the parent language, so we cannot be sure. Linguists have only the descendants of that language to go by, and they make inferences about the parent on the basis of the children, especially the older children like Greek, Latin, and Sanskrit.

ahead, I rashly decided to speed up," the word "I" performs the nominative function (it refers to the one doing the action). Even though the word "I" is not first in the sentence, it is clear that it is the subject because the earlier material is set off by a comma. In a highly inflected Indo-European language, one would perform this "naming" function by putting the subject ("I," in the example above) in the nominative case.

Vocative Function. The word "vocative" comes from the Latin for "to call," and it indicates a particular person or group of people that the sentence is addressing. In English, we often indicate the vocative function by adding the word "o" before the addressee. For example, "O God, please hear our prayer." We also normally set off the addressee by commas, and the commas can sometimes indicate the vocative function without using the word "o." For example, "We pray, God, that you may hear our prayer." In a highly inflected Indo-European language, one could perform this function of "calling" by placing the word referring to the addressee ("God," in this example) in the vocative case.

Accusative Function. The word "accusative" comes from the Latin for "to accuse," which seems to have been a misunderstanding by the Romans of the Greek name for the case.[3] This function is to limit the action of a verb by stating the object to whom or to which that action applies. In the example just above, "O God, please hear our prayer," the word "prayer" is the object of the verb "hear." In English, then, the accusative function is usually performed by placing the object directly after the verb. This function also pertains to prepositions. When the preposition implies an action, as in the example "She goes into the room," the accusative function limits the action of "going" by indicating where she goes. In a highly inflected Indo-European language, one would perform this limiting function by placing the object ("prayer" or "room" in these examples) in the accusative case.

---

3. The Greek name comes from a word that can mean "accusation," but can also mean "cause." The idea may well have been that this is the function of stating the cause of an action, or in other words, the object on whom the action is performed.

Dative Function. The word "dative" comes from the Latin for "given," and this function is to specify the person to whom something is given. More generally, it indicates the person for whose advantage (or disadvantage) any action is performed. In English, one can fulfill the dative function by placing the word immediately after the verb or by using a preposition such as "to," "for," or "on behalf of." For example, consider two sentences: "Jesus forgives us our sins," and "Jesus forgives sins for us." Both sentences indicate a "dative" type of idea, because Jesus' act of forgiving sins brings about an advantage for us. The first (which is better English) uses the placement of the word "us" to perform that function, and the second uses the preposition "for." In a highly inflected Indo-European language, one could perform this function by placing the word ("us," in these examples) in the dative case.

Instrumental Function. This function was not named as such by Greek or Roman grammarians, but has instead been coined in the modern era to describe a function in Greek and Latin, one that remained an actual case in ancient Sanskrit (and, for that matter, in the Slavic languages today). Hence its name is English rather than Latin-based, and it indicates that by whom or by which an action is done. In English this function is normally performed by the preposition "by." For example, "Jesus' advent was foretold by the prophets," or "Jesus healed the man by his divine power." When the action is performed by a person, grammarians call this "agency," and when the action is performed by or through an impersonal force, grammarians call it "means" or "instrument." Thus, one can think of these as separate ideas ("agency" implies that the agent is the one doing the action, but "means" implies that some person uses this impersonal instrument to perform the action) or as variations on the same general function: that by whom or by which something is accomplished. In a highly inflected Indo-European language, one *could* perform this function by placing the word ("prophets" or "power" in these examples) in the instrumental case, but in fact, Greek and Latin do not do this, as we shall see later in this chapter.

Locative Function. The word "locative" is also modern, and this function is to "locate" an action or a state by indicating the place where it occurs. In English one would perform this idea through the preposition "in" or "at." For example, "Peter was executed in Rome," or "Paul preached at the Temple of Apollo in Corinth." In a highly inflected Indo-European language, one could perform this function by placing the word ("Rome," "Temple," or "Corinth" in these examples) in the locative case. Greek and Latin use their locative case rather sparingly, so they also have other ways to indicate this function.

Genitive Function. This word comes from the Latin word for "to beget," and it thus indicates some kind of relationship or belonging between two subjects. More generally, it is the function of indicating to whom or to what larger group a subject belongs. In English, we can perform this function using the possessive case or the preposition "of." For example, in the phrase "David's book," the possessive "David's" indicates the one to whom the book belongs. In the phrase "Lion of the tribe of Judah," the word "of" introduces a prepositional phrase that shows the relationship between the Messiah and the Israelite tribe from which he is descended. In the phrase "Jesus of Nazareth," the word "of" relates Jesus to the place from which he came. In a highly inflected Indo-European language, one could fulfill this relational or belonging function by placing the word ("David," "tribe," or "Nazareth," in these examples) in the genitive case.

Ablative Function. This word comes from the Latin word meaning "to separate," and thus this is the function of separating or distinguishing two subjects. In English, the words "from" and "than" are often used to perform this function, as in the examples "London is very far from New York" and "Ben is taller than Paul." In many cases, the idea of separation or distinction overlaps with the idea of belonging or relationship. For example, to say that Jesus is from the tribe of Judah is at once to link him to the rest of the tribe and to distinguish him from his ancestors and parents. As a result, there is a great deal of variety in the ways Indo-European languages handle the genitive and the ablative functions. I will return to this variety a bit later in this chapter.

Table 4-4   Indo-European Word Relations/Functions

Name of Function	Brief Description
Nominative	Naming a subject
Vocative	Direct address
Accusative	Object of an action
Dative	Subject to or for whom action is done
Instrumental	Subject by whom/which action is done
Locative	Place where action is done or event happens
Genitive	Relationship between subjects; belonging
Ablative	Separation or distinction between subjects

Table 4-4 gives a summary of these eight basic word relations or functions.

In a "perfect" Indo-European language, one might be able to indicate each of these basic kinds of relations through a noun or pronoun in the appropriate case, without needing to rely on either a preposition or word order to convey the relation. As a result, one could use prepositions with these various cases to add greater specificity about the relation between the words, and of course, one could use word order for nuance or emphasis. In contrast, notice that in the English examples I have given, one must ordinarily use either prepositions or word order to perform these functions. So in order to convey more specific relations between words, one has to add more prepositions, and the staggering number of prepositions in English is very daunting to foreigners trying to learn our language. Synthetic languages can convey relations between words without nearly as many prepositions as English has. For example, in English, one needs different prepositions to say "He is in the room" and "She goes into the room." In other languages (like Latin, for example), one can simply use a preposition with one case to indicate the first and the same preposition with another case to indicate the second.

From Indo-European Functions to Greek and Latin Cases

As you have probably guessed, though, there is no "perfect" Indo-European language. All the ancient and modern descendants of the parent language have peculiarities in the way they use their cases. In some instances, one case handles several functions that were probably originally the purview of different cases. In other instances, what had probably been a single function is subdivided into very specific subfunctions and parceled out among various cases. In still other instances (as in English), other grammatical constructions (word order, prepositions) take over the functions of certain cases. Thus, as I have mentioned above, the actual Indo-European languages vary greatly in the number of cases they possess. As you learn Greek or Latin, you will have to learn the specific ways the different cases are used, and in neither language does that case usage exactly match what I have given you in the previous section. Nevertheless, I am convinced that a big-picture understanding of these eight basic functions makes it easier for a student to remember the varied uses of each case in a given Indo-European language like Greek or Latin. The reason for this is that understanding the big picture makes it easier to memorize the details: the student can recognize the pattern behind the details rather than seeing them as unrelated facts to be learned. How, then, are these eight functions parceled out among the actual cases of Greek and Latin?

Answering this question requires a brief foray into the world of professional grammar. You will remember that grammatical categorization is imposed on a language and is arbitrary to some degree. One of the places where the arbitrary nature of grammar shows up is in the classification of cases. Does one classify them by function (as I did in the previous section), or does one classify them by form? In other words, does one call x and y two different cases whenever one identifies two significantly different functions x and y, or does one call them different cases only when, in a given language, x and y usually have a different form? High-level discussions of grammar differ on this question, but most beginning grammar books classify the cases in terms of form. So let us go through our eight basic functions and see how the

Latin and Greek forms perform those functions. Once we have seen this movement, I will schematize this information in different ways with two tables and a figure. You may not grasp all of this the first time you read it, but if you read the discussion a couple of times and study the tables and the figure, you should be able to understand how we get from the Indo-European idea of eight functional relations to the actual cases of Greek and Latin.

In both Latin and Greek, the "naming" and "calling" functions are performed by two distinct cases, so these obviously are called nominative and vocative. In the majority of instances in both languages, however, the form of a noun in the vocative case is the same as the form of a noun in the nominative case. For example, the noun for "daughter" in Latin is *filia* in either the vocative or the nominative case, but the noun for "son" is *fili* in the vocative, but *filius* in the nominative. So the vocative is called a "minor case," and as you learn noun paradigms you will probably not be required to memorize it, since you can recognize *fili* as a vocative, even without having memorized that form. The nominative is a "major case," and you will have to memorize it. If the naming and calling functions had always been performed by words of the same form, then one could have said that the nominative and vocative were identical, and thus that the vocative was not a discrete case. Since, however, there are some instances where the calling function produces a different form, we do say that the vocative is a separate case in Greek and Latin. Similarly, in both Greek and Latin the accusative function is performed by a discrete case of that name. So with respect to the nominative, vocative, and accusative functions, Greek and Latin work the same way. Both possess two major cases (nominative and accusative) and one minor case (vocative) to handle these relations of words.

With respect to the other five kinds of relations, Greek and Latin work differently. In Greek, the dative, locative, and instrumental functions are all performed by words in one case, called the dative. In Latin, on the other hand, the locative function is sometimes (not often) retained as a separate case, and the instrumental function is sometimes performed by the dative case and sometimes by the ablative case. (Latin distinguishes be-

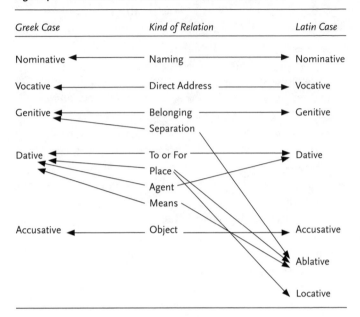

Figure 4-1 Functions and Cases in Greek and Latin

Greek Case	Kind of Relation	Latin Case
Nominative	Naming	Nominative
Vocative	Direct Address	Vocative
Genitive	Belonging	Genitive
	Separation	
Dative	To or For	Dative
	Place	
	Agent	
	Means	
Accusative	Object	Accusative
		Ablative
		Locative

tween a personal agent and an impersonal means, and it normally uses the dative case for the first and the ablative case for the second.) So neither Greek nor Latin retains a distinct instrumental case. Furthermore, Latin uses its locative case quite rarely (mainly only in references to major cities of the Roman world); in most instances the function of that case is carried by a prepositional phrase with the ablative case. So the locative is called a minor case, like the vocative. Furthermore, in Greek the belonging function and the separating/distinguishing function are both performed by words in one case, called the genitive. Figure 4-1 indicates how the basic functions of Indo-European word relations are parceled out among Greek and Latin. You can best make sense of this figure by starting each line in the middle and then working toward the edges (that is, by starting with the function and working toward first the Greek and then the Latin way of performing that function). This figure helps one to recognize that in Greek, the "catch-all" case—the one performing

Table 4-5 From Function to Case in Greek and Latin

Function	Greek Case	Latin Case
Naming a subject	Nominative	Nominative
Direct address	Vocative	Vocative
Object of an action	Accusative	Accusative
Subject to or for whom action is done	Dative	Dative
Subject by whom/which action is done	Dative	Dative/Ablative
Place where action is done	Dative	Locative/Ablative
Relationship between subjects; belonging	Genitive	Genitive
Separation or distinction between subjects	Genitive	Ablative

the most different functions, is the dative. In Latin, the catch-all case is the ablative.

Table 4-5 gives the same information with a different style of presentation. Here you can understand best by starting each line on the left side (with the function) and then working across to the Greek and then to the Latin way of performing that function.

Accordingly, if one classifies cases by form, then Greek has four major cases and one minor case, but Latin has five major cases and two minor cases. In Greek the cases are nominative, vocative (a minor case), genitive (including the separating function), dative (including the locative and instrumental functions), and accusative. In Latin the cases are nominative, vocative (a minor case), genitive, dative (including the instrumental function when the "instrument" is a personal agent), accusative, ablative (including the instrumental function when the "instrument" is an impersonal means, and including the locative function in many instances), and locative (a minor case). Table 4-6 (page 68) gives this information. To understand this table best, you can begin with the case name on the left and then read across to see the different functions of that case in Greek and Latin. Notice that the eight basic functions (eight kinds of relations between words) are covered by five different forms (five cases, the way your grammar book is likely to define cases) in Greek and seven different forms (seven cases) in Latin.

As you learn Greek or Latin, you will constantly be exposed to

Table 4-6   From Case to Function in Greek and Latin

Case	Functions in Greek	Functions in Latin
Nominative	Naming	Naming
Vocative	Direct Address	Direct Address
Genitive	Relationship, belonging; Separation, distinction	Relationship, belonging
Dative	Subject to or for whom action is done; Place; Agent or means	Subject to or for whom action is done; Agent
Accusative	Object of an action	Object of an action
Ablative	——	Separation, distinction; Means; Place
Instrumental	——	——
Locative	——	Place

new uses of various cases. Each time you encounter a new use, I suggest that you try to understand that use as a variation on one of the eight basic case relations I have been discussing. For example, take the comparison that follows: "Ben is taller than Paul." In either Greek or Latin, the word "Ben" would have to be in the nominative case. In both languages, the normal (not the only) way to express "than Paul" would be to put the word "Paul" in a particular case, with no word "than." In Greek, that case would be genitive, but in Latin, it would be ablative. You will learn these uses as something like "genitive of the second member of a comparison" (in Greek) or "ablative of the second member of a comparison" (in Latin). Remembering such a use might be difficult if you just go by that cumbersome description of it, but it will be easy to remember if you recognize that saying "Ben is taller than Paul" has to do with distinguishing Ben from Paul, and that in Latin, the distinguishing/separating function is performed by the ablative case, but in Greek that basic function is performed by the genitive case. Recognizing the big picture of what is happening with cases makes it easier to learn and remember the specific uses your textbook will teach you, because you will be learning these specific uses as variations on a common theme, rather than as seemingly unrelated bits of information.

Anticipating the Memory Work—Declensions in Greek and Latin

Thus far in this chapter, I have used the word "form" a great deal, but I have not yet specified what it means to say that the form of a word changes. In Greek and Latin, words in the inflected word classes (that is, the parts of speech that change in form—nouns, adjectives [including articles], pronouns, and verbs) are formed from **roots**, that is, groups of letters/sounds that convey a basic idea. The languages then add **prefixes** to these roots (letters/sounds on the front of the word) and **suffixes** (letters/sounds on the end of the word). Some of these changes to the root modify the basic idea to form new words. For example, *surgo* in Latin is used in the sense of "to rise," as in the English derivative "surge." *Insurgo* is used to mean "to rise up against," as in the derivative "insurrection." *Resurgo* is often used in the sense of "to rise again," as in the derivative "resurrection." Other changes make the root into one or another part of speech (the same root will usually yield a noun, a verb, an adjective, and an adverb), and still others adapt the word to its different grammatical functions. In the case of nouns (and adjectives, which I will discuss in the next chapter), the changes that adapt the word to different grammatical functions are all suffixes. That is, the beginning of the noun stays the same, but the ending changes to indicate how the word relates to other words. Therefore, as you learn Greek or Latin nouns, you will have to learn the root for each word, how that word is normally used (what most people would call the "meaning" or "definition"), and the various endings that adapt the word to different uses. Grammatically, each noun's form indicates three pieces of information about that noun: its gender, number, and case. We have already covered case, so at this point we need to consider gender and number a bit further.

You may think that the idea of number is obvious, since you

know that a noun can be either singular or plural. You may re-member, however, that when I introduced the idea of case and number at the beginning of this chapter, I added parentheti-cally that the singular/plural distinction is true in English, but not necessarily in other languages. This may be unfathomable to you, because you may think that nothing could be more ba-sic than a distinction between one and more than one. Think, though, about certain everyday objects: Is a pair of trousers sin-gular or plural? Is a couple (a husband and wife) singular or plu-ral? There are certain subjects that are so often considered in pairs that one would be hard-pressed to speak of these as "plu-ral." In order to reflect the fact that certain things come in pairs, rather than in either singular or plural, some languages possess grammatical forms for a **dual** number. So there can be one set of forms for each case in the singular, another set for each case in the dual, and a third set for each case in the plural. (Rarely, the dual number can be used for two of anything, even if those two things do not obviously constitute a natural pair.) If you are about to panic at the thought of learning so many extra forms for each noun, do not despair. In Latin, as in English, there are no dual forms. In Greek there evidently were many dual forms in the language's early history, but even by the time of Homer (late eighth century B.C.) these forms were becoming relatively rare. In Attic Greek from the classical period (fifth and fourth centuries B.C.), there are few such forms, and there are none in the New Testament (first century A.D.). Dual forms do reappear in some patristic Greek writings (second through eighth centu-ries A.D.), since the authors sought to emulate the high style of Attic Greek, but such forms are not common. My favorite ex-ample is the phrase "one out of both" to refer to the fact that Christ is both divine and human. The Greek word for "both" ἀμφοῖν [amphoin] is a dual form. Few beginning Greek students are asked to learn the dual forms, although textbooks of classi-cal Greek usually include them for reference. So even though you are unlikely to have to memorize dual forms and unlikely to encounter them very often, recognizing that they exist (or at least used to exist) can serve to remind you that there are vari-ous ways to express ideas. One may consider "two" as "plural" or as something between singular and plural, and neither one of these is more logical or "right" than the other.[4]

Another concept that needs explanation is **gender**. This may be a surprising concept to English speakers, because in English, there is no such thing as purely grammatical gender. If a word refers to a man, a boy, or (in some cases) a male animal, it is considered **masculine**, and the pronoun "he" refers to it. If it refers to a woman, a girl, or (again, only in some cases) a female animal, it is considered **feminine**, and the pronoun "she" refers to it. In most other cases, the object or idea is considered **neuter**, and the pronoun "it" refers to it. (There are a few exceptions, such as referring to the Christian Church or to a ship as "she," rather than "it.") In most other languages, grammatical gender is different from and often unrelated to actual maleness or femaleness. Some languages (like French) have no grammatically neuter words—all are masculine or feminine. Most European languages have words of all three genders, but in all except English, a word can be grammatically masculine or feminine even if it obviously refers to a thing, rather than to a male or female. For example, in Greek and Latin, the words for the abstract virtues (wisdom, goodness, justice) are all grammatically feminine and are thus referred to as "she" rather than "it." Therefore, when you learn a Greek or Latin noun, you will have to learn what grammatical gender the word is (in both languages, masculine, feminine, and neuter words are present) as well as what the word's root is and how it is used. This will be part of learning vocabulary.

Accordingly, if a given Greek noun possesses all the possible forms (that is, if it has dual forms as well as singular and plural), there will be fifteen forms of that word, all identifiable by the ending (suffix) following the root. There will be five endings for the five cases in the singular, five for the same five cases

---

4. If you have the privilege of learning Hebrew, as well, you will find that biblical Hebrew does have dual forms, and you do have to learn them. My favorite example is that the word for Egypt (*Mitzrayim*) is dual in form, because the people of Israel thought of Egypt as being a natural pair of two parts: Lower Egypt (the Nile delta, where the Hebrews lived during their sojourn in Egypt) and Upper Egypt (the southern part of the country, upstream).

in the dual, and five for the same cases in the plural. Of these fifteen, you will probably be asked to learn eight—the singular and plural endings for the nominative, genitive, dative, and accusative cases. Similarly, a given Latin noun will have fourteen different endings (seven cases each for singular and plural), and of these, you will probably be asked to learn ten (singular and plural endings for the nominative, genitive, dative, accusative, and ablative cases). Furthermore, each noun will have a specific grammatical gender that you will have to learn.

The forms of each noun (and adjective) generally fall into one or another of several patterns, called **declensions**. (To change the form of a noun, adjective, or pronoun is to **decline** it, a word obviously related to "declension.") Greek has three declensions, that is, three distinct patterns of endings, and Latin has five declensions of nouns. When you learn a vocabulary word, you will need to learn its declension, since that will be your key to producing and recognizing the forms. In both Greek and Latin, most first-declension nouns are feminine, most second-declension nouns are masculine or neuter, and there are third-declension nouns of all three genders. In Latin, there are fourth-declension nouns of all three genders as well, and most fifth-declension nouns are feminine. (Greek has no fourth or fifth declension.) Therefore, we can see that a beginning Latin student has more to learn in connection with nouns than a beginning Greek student does: Latin nouns have two more cases than Greek, and there are five patterns rather than three. (If you are studying Latin, do not despair yet. The Latin verb system is extensive, but not as daunting as the Greek verb system.)

As you study Greek or Latin, you will gradually be introduced to all the paradigms of nouns, just as you are gradually introduced to the specific case usages. Armed with your growing knowledge of the endings and your expanding vocabulary, you will be able to look at a given word, identify its gender, declension, and basic usage from the information you memorized when you learned it as a vocabulary word, identify its case and number from your knowledge of the endings for that declension, and thus understand how it is used in the sentence. This task of identifying the various features of each noun (basic usage, declension, gender, number, and case) will be slow and cumbersome at first, but with practice you will build this skill to the point that you can make these identifications rapidly and almost unconsciously. This is called **parsing** a noun—identifying the pieces of information that the word and its form convey—and parsing is one of the most basic skills involved in reading a sentence in a highly inflected language like Latin or Greek.

As an example of what is involved in parsing nouns, consider the following sentence from Paul's treatment of sin in Romans 3. Verse 20 (the conclusion of that discussion) reads as follows in English: "For no human being will be justified in his sight by works of the law, since through the law comes knowledge of sin." Let us look at one phrase and one clause from that sentence, since you have already learned enough to understand how the phrase and the clause work. The phrase translated "by works of the law" in English is actually ἐξ ἔργων νόμου [ex ergōn nomou] in the Greek New Testament, and the Latin Vulgate renders this as *ex operibus legis*. Notice several things here. First, Greek, Latin, and English all express this idea with a prepositional phrase. In fact, Greek and Latin even use the same preposition, ἐξ/ex (a Greek preposition that was taken into the Latin language), a fact that serves to remind us that these are in fact quite similar languages. Second, the idea of this prepositional phrase "by works" is one of separation or origin. Justification does not "come out of" works. So if one thinks about case usage in Indo-European languages in general, this is an ablative idea, but in Greek, the ablative function is assumed by the genitive case. So you expect to find the word "works" in the genitive plural in Greek, but in the ablative plural in Latin, and this is exactly what you have: ἔργων [ergōn] is genitive plural, and *operibus* is ablative plural. Third, the phrase "of the law" in English expresses a "belonging" kind of idea. What kind of works are we talking about? We are talking about specific works that belong to the general category of the commandments in the Old Testament law. So you would expect the word for "law" to be in the genitive case, and it is, in both languages: νόμου [nomou] in Greek and *legis* in Latin are both genitive singular. Furthermore, you can recognize that in Greek and Latin you do not need a preposition "of" the way you do in English, since the genitive case itself conveys this idea.

Now look at the clause "through the law comes knowledge of sin." In Greek this is διὰ νόμου ἐπίγνωσις ἁμαρτίας [*dia nomou epignōsis hamartias*], and in Latin it is *per legem cognitio peccati*. Once you learn the vocabulary words, you recognize that in neither Greek nor Latin does this clause have a verb. The word "comes" is added by the English translators because in English, one has to have a verb in order to have a clause. In Greek and Latin, by contrast, one can have a clause if one simply has a subject ("knowledge of sin") and a predicate "[is] through the law." If "knowledge of sin" is the subject, then why is it placed last in the clause? Because word order is not crucial in Greek and Latin. We recognize that "knowledge" is the subject because it is in the nominative case. In Greek, ἐπίγνωσις [*epignōsis*] is a third-declension feminine noun, and it is nominative singular. In Latin, we have the same situation: *cognitio* is also a third-declension feminine noun that is nominative singular. Similarly, the idea "of sin" is expressed in both languages by a noun in the genitive singular (ἁμαρτίας [*hamartias*] in Greek; *peccati* in Latin), and in both languages, the idea "through the law" is expressed by a prepositional phrase. Greek and Latin conceive of this prepositional idea differently, however. To the Greek mind, διά [*dia*] ("through") is an ablative kind of idea, an idea of separation or distinction, so the object of that preposition (νόμου [*nomou*]) goes in the genitive case (remember again that Greek has no ablative forms). To the Latin mind, on the other hand, *per* ("through") is a spatial kind of idea, as if the knowledge actually moves toward us by coming through the medium of the law, so in Latin the object of the preposition (*legem*) goes in the accusative case. Here we see that within the basic structure given by the eight Indo-European word relations, each language is free to construe various ideas in its own way. To say that the object of the preposition "through" should be in the accusative case in Latin but in the genitive case in Greek sounds rather arbitrary, but behind this apparent arbitrariness lies a different way of thinking about ideas. As always, you do have to memorize which case goes with which preposition, but there is an inner logic to the match between a preposition and the case of its object that you can recognize if you think about this situation in light of the general functions of cases we examined earlier in this chapter.

Thus we see that in a relatively simple sentence like this one, there are some ideas that Greek, Latin, and English all express the same way and others that Greek and Latin express similarly to each other, but differently from English. We also see some slight differences between Greek and Latin, and recognizing these differences can give us a small window into some of the differences between the ways Greeks and Romans understood reality around them. Perhaps more important for your purposes, this sentence gives you an idea of what is involved in reading Greek or Latin. Understanding a sentence entails (among other things) learning the declension, the root, and the basic usage of each noun; then parsing each noun's form by giving its gender, number, and case; then recognizing how that form links the noun to the other words in the sentence.

With this basic introduction to nouns and cases behind us, it is time to turn to other words in Greek and Latin that are closely related to nouns—adjectives, articles, and pronouns. These will be the subjects of the next chapter.

APPENDIX: GRAMMATICAL TERMS INTRODUCED IN CHAPTER 4

Ablative function/case: The function of distinguishing or separating one word from another. Latin has an ablative case, but in Greek the ablative function is performed by the genitive case.

Accusative function/case: The function of limiting the action of a verb or the idea of a preposition by indicating the object of that action/idea. Both Greek and Latin have an accusative case to perform this function. In both Greek and Latin, however, sometimes objects (especially objects of prepositions) can be in other cases besides the accusative.

Case: The name for a particular form of a noun, pronoun, adjective, or article, when that form serves to show how the word is related to the rest of the sentence.

Dative function/case: The function of indicating to whom, for whom, to what, or for what the action of a sentence is done. Both Greek and Latin have a dative case to perform this function.

Declension: A pattern for producing the case forms of a given noun or adjective. Latin has five declensions of nouns, and Greek has three. In the case of adjectives, Greek and Latin both have two patterns. (One pattern uses first- and second-declension endings, and the other uses third-declension endings.)

Decline: To make the necessary changes to a noun, pronoun, adjective, or article, so as to produce the forms needed for the various cases, genders, and numbers.

Dual number: A set of forms used in early Greek to denote two of a given object. In many cases, dual forms existed for nouns that described natural pairs and that were thus not considered to be either singular or plural (e.g., "trousers"). Latin has no dual number.

Feminine gender: A grammatical concept that dictates that a noun and the words that modify it will use feminine forms. Feminine gender is not necessarily connected to whether the subject being described is actually female.

First-person pronoun: The pronoun that refers to the person speaking or writing the sentence (e.g., "I," "mine," "me," "we," "ours," "us" in English).

Gender: A purely grammatical concept that dictates which forms a noun and the words that modify it will use. Gender is not necessarily connected to whether the subject being described is actually male, female, or inanimate. Greek and Latin both have three grammatical genders: masculine, feminine, and neuter.

Genitive function/case: The function of indicating a particular kind of relation, relationship, or belonging between a word and the rest of the sentence. Greek and Latin both have a genitive case to perform this function.

Instrumental function/case: The function of indicating the agent, means, or instrument by whom or by which an action is accomplished. Neither Greek nor Latin has an instrumental case. In Greek, the dative case performs the instrumental function. In Latin the dative or ablative case can perform this function.

Locative function/case: The function of locating the place where the event of a sentence happens. In Greek there is no locative case, and the dative case performs this function. In Latin, a locative case is used to indicate location with some nouns, but most of the time the ablative case performs this function.

Masculine gender: A grammatical concept that dictates that a noun and the words that modify it will use masculine forms. Masculine gender is not necessarily connected to whether the subject being described is actually male.

Neuter gender: A grammatical concept that dictates that a noun and the words that modify it will use neuter forms. Neuter gender is not necessarily connected to whether the subject being described is actually inanimate.

Nominative function/case: The function of naming a person, place, object, or idea. Greek and Latin both have a nominative case to perform this function.

Number: The grammatical concept for indicating how many subjects one is describing. Latin conceives of number in terms of either singular or plural. Early Greek conceives of number in terms of singular, dual, or plural, but later Greek almost always uses plural forms for dual subjects.

Parse: To identify the relevant grammatical information conveyed by the form of a word (e.g., the Latin word *hominum* is genitive [case], masculine [gender], plural [number]).

Plural number: A set of forms indicating that a noun, pronoun, verb, adjective, or article refers to more than one subject (e.g., "men" rather than "man").

Prefix: Letters added to the front of a word to produce different forms.

Root: The basic part of a word, indicating how the word is used (that is, conveying the word's meaning). Prefixes and suffixes are added to the root to produce different forms. The root changes as well in some forms.

Second-person pronoun: The pronoun that refers to the person to whom the speaker is speaking or the writer is writing (e.g., "thou," "thine," "thee," "ye," "yours," "you" in English).

Singular number: A set of forms indicating that a noun, pronoun, verb, adjective, or article refers to a single subject (e.g., "man" rather than "men").

Suffix: Letters added to the end of a word to produce different forms.

Third-person pronoun: The pronoun that refers to some other person or object besides the speaker/writer or the hearer/reader (e.g., "she," "hers," "her," "he," "his," "him," "it," "its," "they," "theirs," "them" in English).

Vocative function/case: The function of identifying whom the speaker/writer is addressing in the sentence (e.g., "O *God,* we pray that you may hear us"). Greek and Latin both have a vocative case, but its form is often the same as the form of the nominative case.

5

ADJECTIVES, ARTICLES, AND PRONOUNS

In the previous chapter we saw that when a noun changes form (in the classical languages, it adds different suffixes or endings) to assume different cases, grammarians say that the noun is "declined." In Greek and Latin, nouns are not the only words that decline. Pronouns assume different cases, as well (which should not be too surprising, since pronouns are the only words in English that still exhibit different case forms), and so do adjectives. Furthermore, in Greek the article (equivalent to "the" in English) assumes different cases, as well. (Latin does not have an article.) The fact that all of these words decline may raise questions in the mind of an English speaker. Why do articles need case endings? Why do adjectives need case endings? How can anyone communicate in a language that does not have a word for "a" or "the"? In this chapter, let us examine these questions by looking first at adjectives, then at articles, and finally at pronouns. In the process of treating these three groups of words,[1] we will see more clearly some of the advantages of a highly inflected language in communicating ideas clearly.

Adjectives and the Advantages of Declining Them

An English speaker might be forgiven for thinking that there is no reason to decline adjectives. After all, even if it is okay to

---

1. I do not call these groups "word classes" or "parts of speech," because in English categorization, articles are not a formal word class, but are a subcategory of adjectives. In Greek and Latin classification, adjectives are not a

decline nouns (something an English speaker may not be willing to grant), why does one also need to decline the adjectives that modify them? Why cannot the case of the noun identify its function, and then the adjective can just go with the noun? Of course, it can work that way. After all, many languages (like English) get by well enough without declining either nouns or adjectives, so if one can do that, then one can probably get by declining only nouns, but not adjectives. Nevertheless, there are two distinct advantages to declining adjectives, and I would like to consider each advantage in turn.

First, if an adjective has case forms, those forms aid the reader/hearer in understanding which noun or pronoun the adjective modifies. Consider Jesus' statement from Mark 8:38: "Whoever is ashamed of me and of my words in this adulterous and sinful generation, of him will the Son of Man also be ashamed when he comes in the glory of his Father with the holy angels." In this sentence, the adjectives "adulterous" and "sinful" modify "generation," and in English the adjectives go directly in front of the noun to make it clear that they modify that noun. In both Greek and Latin, however, the words translated "adulterous" and "sinful" in this sentence follow the noun "generation"; they do not precede it. Such placement is rather uncommon in both languages (especially in Latin),[2] but because the adjectives are in the same case as the noun (in Greek they are dative, and in Latin they are ablative), there is no ambiguity at all. Declining adjectives helps clarify the relations between the adjectives and the nouns, which in turn gives the speaker or writer more flexibility to compose the sentence in one order or another for emphasis.

Second, adjectives are not always used to modify nouns.

---

formal word class, but are a subcategory of nouns. Be that as it may, adjectives, articles, and pronouns are discernibly different groups of words.

2. In Greek this is called "long-form attributive word order," in which the adjectives follow the noun but are marked off by articles. Literally, this phrase translates as "the generation this the adulterous and sinful." The repetition of the article "the" helps to show that the adjectives go with the noun in front of them. The shorter form of attributive word order (in this case it would be "the adulterous and sinful generation this") is more common. Because Latin has no articles, it is much less able to handle long-form attributive word order than Greek is, so this construction is rare in Latin.

Sometimes they are used *as* nouns. Remember that in chapter 3, I defined a substantive as any word or phrase that can refer to a person, place, thing, or idea. In Greek, Latin, and English, adjectives can be used substantively, and when they are, having case and number endings on the adjectives enables one to indicate clearly to whom or to what they refer. Consider 1 Peter 3:18, in which Peter asserts, "Christ also died for sins once for all, the righteous for the unrighteous, that he might bring us to God." In this passage, "righteous" and "unrighteous" are adjectives used substantively. "Righteous" means "the righteous one" and refers to Christ, of course. "Unrighteous" means "the unrighteous *ones*" and refers to the many who are not righteous on their own. How then does one know that one of these adjectives is meant to stand for one person and the other for many people? How do we know that the first one is singular and the second one is plural? In English, the only way we can know this is by the context of the passage, because English does not even have singular and plural forms for adjectives, let alone case forms. Grammatically, this passage is ambiguous in English, and it is only through context and our knowledge of what the rest of the New Testament states about Christ's death that we can recognize that "unrighteous" refers to many people. In Greek and Latin, there is no such ambiguity. In both languages, "righteous" (δίκαιος [*dikaios*] in Greek, *iustus* in Latin) is nominative masculine singular and clearly refers to Christ, since in the previous clause, "Christ" is nominative masculine singular. In both languages, "unrighteous" (ἀδικῶν [*adikōn*] in Greek, *iniustis* in Latin) is plural, although not surprisingly, in Greek the adjective is genitive, whereas in Latin it is ablative. Declining adjectives enables one to make crystal-clear that the death of the one righteous man takes the place of the many unrighteous people. In English, one cannot make this clear unless one adds the word "one" to "righteous" and "ones" or "many" to "unrighteous."

Thus we can see that there are definite advantages to declining adjectives, and so we can perhaps appreciate the fact that Greek and Latin do so, even if it means that we have additional forms to learn. You may be wondering at this point how many adjective forms you are going to have to learn. Obviously, a given noun can be only masculine, feminine, or neuter (not all three), but each adjective will need to have masculine, feminine, *and* neuter forms so that it can modify a noun of any gender. This means that a fully declined Greek adjective would have forms for singular, dual, and plural number, for five cases, and for three genders. This would make forty-five forms, and of these you will probably need to learn twenty-four (two numbers, four cases, three genders). A fully declined Latin adjective would have two numbers, seven cases, and three genders, or forty-two forms, of which you will most likely need to learn thirty (two numbers, five cases, and three genders). Thus, the bad news is that you have a lot more forms to learn for an adjective than for a noun.

Nevertheless, the good news is that learning to decline adjectives does not involve learning very many new forms at all, because in most cases, Greek and Latin adjectives use the same endings as the corresponding nouns do. In both Greek and Latin, there are two basic patterns of adjectives, and you can recognize these patterns when you remember that in both languages, most first-declension nouns are feminine, most second-declension nouns are masculine or neuter, and there are third-declension nouns of all three genders. Thus, one pattern of adjectives uses first-declension endings for its feminine forms and second-declension endings for its masculine and neuter forms, and so adjectives of this pattern are called "first/second-declension adjectives." The other pattern of adjectives uses third-declension endings for all three genders, and thus these are called "third-declension adjectives."[3] So once you have learned the endings for nouns, you will be well on your way toward being able to recognize adjective forms, as well.[4] For Latin students, it is also heartening to learn that there are no adjectives using fourth- or fifth-declension endings. Even though Latin has five declensions of nouns instead of three, it still has only two basic paradigms of adjectives—no more than Greek has.

---

3. There are some adjectives in Greek that use third-declension endings in the masculine and neuter, but first-declension endings in the feminine. These are relatively rare. There are also a few common adjectives that are irregular in both Greek and Latin.

4. This was part of the reason the Greeks and Romans did not consider adjectives to be a separate word class.

This might be a good place for a word of warning. In both of the classical languages, third-declension nouns and adjectives exhibit a good deal more variety than first- and second-declension nouns and adjectives do. In one respect, however, third-declension adjectives are easier than first- and second-declension adjectives, because in many instances, they use the same form for both masculine and feminine. In any event, it is not difficult to recognize the forms of adjectives once one has learned the noun forms well.

Articles—Using the Ones You Have and Working Around the Ones You Do Not Have

In chapter 3 we saw that English has both a definite article (the word "the") and an indefinite article ("a" or "an"). These articles are used to specify how the following noun is to be understood. For example, are we speaking of any book, or of a particular book? If we are speaking of any book, we use the indefinite article—"*a* book." If we are speaking of a particular book, we indicate that fact with the definite article—"*the* book." In English, we use articles voluminously, and it is thus hard for English speakers to imagine life without them.[5]

Let us look more carefully at our copious use of articles in English, so as to gain some clues about how other languages can do without one or both of them. First, recognize that we use nouns in three ways: with the definite article, with the indefinite article, or with no article. When we use a noun with the definite article or the indefinite article, we are thinking of the thing that noun refers to as a concrete sort of entity, but when we use it with no article, we are thinking of that noun as an abstract quality. So nouns that obviously refer to concrete entities are not normally used without an article unless they are in the plural.

5. As an example of how common articles are in English, and thus how daunting it is for a foreigner to learn to use them correctly, consider that when my Russian-speaking friends write in English, they can rarely compose even one sentence that has no mistakes in article use. Russian has no articles at all, and so the nuances of using articles in English—nuances you take for granted without even considering them—are virtually beyond the comprehension of even very good Russian students learning English.

We speak of "*a* book" (any book, not one particular book), of "*the* book" (this or that particular book), or even of "books" in the plural without an article. We do not say "book" in the singular without an article, because "book" refers to something concrete, and we use articles, numbers, or the plural to indicate concrete things. In contrast, if the noun in question refers to an abstract quality, we generally use it only in the singular, and without an article. We speak of "wisdom," but not of "a wisdom" or of "wisdoms," and not usually of "the wisdom," unless we are referring to a specific, more concrete kind of wisdom, as in the phrase "the wisdom given to me by God." Even with the word "virtue" itself, if we are referring to the idea in general, we say "virtue," whereas if we are talking about a particular virtuous quality (or several such qualities), we can say "a virtue," "the virtue of kindness," and "virtues." We use nouns with articles to refer to concrete, specific realities, and we use nouns without articles to refer to more abstract generalities. In English there are some nouns (like "virtue") that can be used both ways, but most nouns (like "book") are used one way or the other. How, then, can a language get by without both definite and indefinite articles? I will have to answer this question separately for Greek and Latin, because this is one of the places where the two languages diverge.

The Definite Article in Greek

In Greek, which has a definite article but not an indefinite one, the abstract virtues (ideas that we consider in general, without an article) are considered to be concrete realities. In the Greek mind, wisdom is not an abstraction at all. It is a definite reality here on earth that reflects a higher reality—either the reality of an ideal world (as in Plato's philosophy) or the reality of God who gave us that wisdom (as in the Greek Christian understanding, and to some degree in the neo-Platonic philosophical understanding). Therefore, "wisdom" in Greek is written with the article (ἡ σοφία [*hē sophia*], "*the* wisdom"), a fact that emphasizes the concrete reality of the virtue called "wisdom." Moreover, Greek even uses the article with names: "the Socrates," "the Jesus," "the Paul." In a worldview that does not really include the idea of abstractions, but functions in the realm of the concrete, one does not need three ways to refer to a noun (*"the* virtue," *"a* virtue," and simply "virtue"). One is perfectly able to function with two ways to refer to a noun. So in Greek, preceding a noun with the definite article corresponds to our referring to the noun with the definite article in English (a concrete definite reference), and using a noun with no article corresponds, generally, to our using the indefinite article in English (a concrete indefinite reference). Since the Greeks generally consider even the "abstract" virtues to be concrete realities, they have no concept that corresponds to our use of a noun without an article. This, then, is how the Greeks function without an indefinite article. They are simply not trying to say what we normally mean when we refer to a noun without an article, so when they do not use an article, that corresponds to what we mean when we use the indefinite article. If they say simply "wisdom," that means something like "some kind of wisdom," but if they say "the wisdom," that means wisdom as a concrete manifestation of a higher reality.

The very fact that we refer in English to "good," "evil," "wisdom," "love," and "hatred" in such an abstract way could say something about our mentality. We may be distancing ourselves from these qualities to some degree by the way we refer to them. "Good" is not so much a reality as an unattainable ideal, an abstraction. Conversely, "evil" is not so concrete, and not so much our fault; it is something "out there," away from us. The Greek worldview does not let us treat virtues and vices in this way. They are real. "Goodness" is not an abstraction "out there" somewhere; it is the embodiment in us of God's own character. The Greek language is perhaps better equipped to remind people of this than English is. When we are speaking English, we might do well to take a cue from the Greeks and consciously remind ourselves and others that we are talking about wisdom, virtue, love, as specific, concrete qualities.

To return to grammar, I should point out at this point that the previous paragraphs give only part of the story. In many cases, the presence or absence of a definite article in Greek has more significance as a grammatical marker than it does as an indication of whether the Greeks mean "a" or "the." For example, when a sentence consists of a subject, a verb, and a predicate nominative, the definite article usually marks the subject to distinguish it from the predicate nominative. John 1:1 declares, "The Word was God." In Greek the order is reversed, and "God" comes first: θεὸς ἦν ὁ λόγος [theos ēn ho logos]. Does this mean that in Greek, the sentence says, "God was the Word"? No, because the article (ὁ [ho]) is included with "Word" (λόγος [logos]), but not with "God" (θεός [theos]), thus showing that "Word" is the subject.

In more complicated constructions (especially in classical Greek or the patristic Greek written in imitation of it), the article might go at the beginning of a phrase, the noun that the article modifies at the end of the phrase, and various other modifiers, such as prepositional phrases, in the middle. The article and its noun thus serve very elegantly to bracket the phrase and enable the reader/hearer to see where the modifiers go. For example, the fifth-century Greek Church father Cyril of Alexandria was fond of referring to Christ as ὁ κατ᾽ ἀλήθειαν Υἱός [ho kat' alētheian Huios]. This phrase begins with the article (ὁ [ho]), then it has a prepositional phrase (κατ᾽ ἀλήθειαν [kat' alētheian]), and then a noun (Υἱός [Huios]). Thus, it means "the according-to-truth Son," and I have seen it translated into English way too literally as "the in-truth Son." Of course, in better English, we have to say something like "the one who is truly Son," or perhaps simply "the true Son," although the second of those does not carry as much force as the Greek expression does. In contrast to English, which must either be so literal as to be humorous ("the in-truth Son"), precise but a bit cumbersome ("the one who is truly Son"), or elegant but a bit less forceful ("the true Son"), in Greek the article (ὁ [ho]) goes with the noun (Υἱός [Huios]), and one knows instantly that everything in between modifies the same noun. One can combine elegance, simplicity, and forcefulness quite easily.

As you progress in Greek, you will learn a variety of purely grammatical uses such as these for the article. For now, you should recognize that the presence of a definite article either marks a noun out in some grammatically distinct way or identifies that noun as a concrete reality, and the latter of these corresponds to our use of "the" in front of a concrete noun. The use of a noun without an article in Greek more or less corresponds to our use of the word "a" or "an" with a noun. Our use of certain nouns without any article takes the place of, without actually being equivalent to, the Greek use of the definite article with what they would call a concrete noun (but we would call it an abstract noun).

The definite article in Greek is declined somewhat like a first- and second-declension adjective, although it does not use exactly the same endings as the nouns and adjectives do. You will have to learn the masculine, feminine, and neuter forms for (probably) four cases (out of five), and, of course, both singular and plural.

Communicating without Articles in Latin

If it is now comprehensible how Greek can function with a definite article but not an indefinite one, how can Latin function with no articles at all? Here we need to recognize that originally in the parent Indo-European language, the words that would one day become articles in Greek and in the modern Germanic and Romance languages started out as pronouns. Originally, life went on quite normally in this language family without articles, and articles were a relatively late introduction to the linguistic scene. Consider, for example, that the words for "the" in French, Italian, and Spanish come from the Latin pronoun translated "that one," whose masculine nominative singular form is *ille* (from which one arrives at the French *le* by dropping the beginning of the word, the Italian *il* by dropping the end, and the Spanish *el* by dropping the end and changing the vowel slightly), and whose feminine nominative singular form is *illa* (from which one gets *la* in French, Italian, and Spanish by dropping the beginning of the word). In these languages, the definite article does not even derive from older definite articles (the Greek and Germanic definite articles bear no relation to the French and Spanish articles); it derives from a Latin pronoun. This mini-lesson in linguistic history reminds us that articles are not essential to communication. If a language does not have them, it can make up for the deficiency by having more pronouns and using them more frequently.

This is precisely what Latin does. In many cases where Greek or English would use the definite article, Latin conveys much the same idea by using a pronoun equivalent to "this" or "that." In some cases, Greek might use the definite article with a verb form, and Latin and English would recast the sentence to use a pronoun. For example, John 1:12 states, "To all who received him, who believed in his name, he gave power to become children of God." In Greek, the phrase translated "who believed" consists of the definite article τοῖς [tois], followed by a participle πιστεύουσιν [pisteuousin], so the phrase actually means "the believing [ones]." On the other hand, Latin has difficulty saying "the believing ones" because it has no article, so the Vulgate adds a pronoun and changes the participle to a different verb form, so that the phrase (now a clause) reads *his qui credunt,* which translates as "these who believe." *His* is the masculine dative plural form of the pronoun/adjective *hic,* and this pronoun enables Latin to work around the fact that it does not have an article and therefore cannot easily say "the believing ones." Notice that in this instance, Latin is much more like English than Greek is, in spite of the lack of a definite article. Latin uses a pronoun and a clause in many cases where Greek uses an article and a participle, and in English, we use a construction similar to the Latin one, not at all like the Greek one.

In other instances, Greek identifies a noun concretely by using a definite article, and then specifies what is significant about that noun with a descriptive phrase or clause after it. In these cases, Latin is able to manage without adding a pronoun, because the descriptive clause that follows the noun shows the reader/hearer that the noun has a specific reference. For example, John 1:9 describes Christ as follows: "The true light that enlightens every man was coming into the world." In the Greek for this sentence, the article "the" indicates that John is writing not about any sort of light, but specifically about a definite light, *the* light. Furthermore, the clause following the noun, "that enlightens every man," also serves to identify that light concretely.

So in this case, there are two ways in which the word for light is rendered concrete. Latin is able to use one of these ways—the clause "that enlightens every man"—and considers that to be a sufficient way of identifying the light concretely. Therefore, in this case Latin does not feel the need to add a pronoun in front of the word for "light," and in the Vulgate the sentence reads the equivalent of "True light that enlightens every man was coming into the world." Notice that in this case, Greek and English work more similarly (with a definite article and a clause to render the noun concrete), and Latin works slightly differently (with only the clause) because of its lack of an article.

So as students of Latin, you should recognize that in some cases, you will need to render Latin pronouns (or pronouns used as adjectives) with the definite article in English, and in other cases, you will need to supply the definite article in English, in cases where the context shows that the Latin noun is meant concretely. Be that as it may, Latin is able to function quite well with no articles at all, although the presence of a definite article in Greek often enables it to express ideas more succinctly than Latin can. Because Latin has to use pronouns more often than Greek to make up for its lack of an article, it should not come as a surprise to you that Latin has more pronouns than Greek. I now turn to a discussion of that word class.

Pronouns

As we have already seen in chapter 3, pronouns are words that take the place of nouns. By replacing nouns, the pronouns streamline communication considerably and add elegance to the sentence. Without them, many nouns would have to be repeated over and over again, and communication would be much clumsier. The issue we need to consider here is that of when pronouns replace a noun—in what situations they are used. In general, pronouns in Greek and Latin are used similarly to the way they are used in English, although Latin has to use them more often, because it does not have an article. In this section, I would like to look at six different situations in which pronouns smooth the path to good communication by replacing nouns. For each pronoun, you will need to learn masculine, feminine, and neuter forms for singular and plural and for each of the cases.

Indicating the Speaker/Writer, the Audience, or a Third Party

Consider the following imaginary situation: Nathan is talking to Susan about a mutual friend named Chris. Notice the italicized pronouns in their dialogue. Nathan says, "*I* haven't seen Chris in a long time. Do *you* think *he* is out of town?" Susan responds, "*I* just heard from *him* yesterday. *He* said to tell *you* 'hi' and to let *you* know that *he* has just been really busy with *his* job." In this very simple interchange, there are ten pronouns, all referring to either the speaker, the listener, or the third party (Chris). Now look at the same dialogue as it would have to be spoken if English had no pronouns. Nathan, says, "Nathan hasn't seen Chris in a long time. Does Susan think Chris is out of town?" Susan responds, "Susan just heard from Chris yesterday. Chris said to tell Nathan 'hi' and to let Nathan know that Chris has just been really busy with Chris's job." The second interchange is much more cumbersome, and in some cases, it could even be confusing. When Nathan refers to himself by name, it sounds like he is talking about someone else, rather than about himself. The same effect is produced when Susan refers to herself by name. Without pronouns, a language would be forced into a great deal of repetitive noun usage that would slow down communication considerably.[6]

In this situation, as you already know from chapter 4, the pronouns that speed communication are called **personal pronouns**. These pronouns refer to either the first person (the speaker/writer—"I" or "we"), the second person (the hearer/reader—"you"), or the third person (someone or something else—"he," "she,"

6. It is worth noting here that, as young children begin to talk, they are able to grasp the concrete concepts of names referring to a particular person much sooner than they are able to understand the way pronouns refer to persons. So to aid their children's ability to communicate, parents often address their children by saying their names, rather than using the pronoun "you." I used to say to my son, "Does Trey want more milk?" and he would answer, "Yes, Trey wants milk." This way of communicating is simpler and thus easier for a child to learn, but it is very cumbersome.

"it," or "they"). In English, a personal pronoun is necessary to indicate the subject of a verb whenever that subject is not expressed in another way. One cannot say "is writing a book" in English. One has to specify *who* is writing, either by naming a person ("Susan," for example) or using a pronoun (for instance, "she"). In Greek and Latin, the form of the verb itself includes the idea of a subject, so *scribo* alone in Latin or γράφω [*graphō*] alone in Greek means "I am writing." Because one does not need to use a pronoun to express the verb's subject in the classical languages, if one chooses to do so, it adds emphasis to that subject. Thus *ego scribo* in Latin or ἐγὼ γράφω [*egō graphō*] in Greek would be an emphatic way of saying "I am writing," as if one meant, "I—not another person—am the one who is writing." Thus, in Greek and Latin, the personal pronouns sometimes function as **intensive pronouns**. Greek has personal/intensive pronouns for first person (ἐγώ [*egō*]), second person (σύ [*su*]), and third person (αὐτός [*autos*]). Latin has personal/intensive pronouns for first person (*ego*) and second person (*tu*), but not for third person. Instead, Latin uses its various other pronouns to replace the third-person pronoun. That is, instead of saying "he did this" or "she did this," Latin says the equivalent of "this one did this" or "that one did this." Latin also has a stronger intensive pronoun, *ipse* ("the same one" or "the very one himself/herself").

Referring Back to the Subject of the Clause

Consider this sentence: "He hit himself in the thumb with a hammer." Of course, if English had no pronouns, one would have to say, "Stephen hit Stephen," which would be clear but awkward. If one had only personal pronouns, one could say, "He hit him," which would be ambiguous. In this case, did Stephen hit Stephen with the hammer, or did he hit another male person with the hammer? In order to provide both clarity and elegance, a language needs **reflexive pronouns**, which refer back to the subject of the sentence or clause in which they occur. English, Greek, and Latin all have these reflexive pronouns.

Because these pronouns refer to a previously stated subject, they cannot be used in the nominative case. (One could not say "sheself" in English.) In Greek, as in contemporary English, there are separate forms for the first person (ἐμαυτοῦ [*emautou*]— "myself"), the second person (σεαυτοῦ [*seautou*]—"yourself"), and the third person (ἑαυτοῦ [*heautou*]—"himself" or "herself"). In Latin, only third-person forms exist (*sui*), and the personal pronouns serve reflexively in the first and second persons. In other words, in Latin, one would say, "I hit *me* with a hammer" (which used to be common in English, as in the bedtime prayer "Now I lay *me* down to sleep"), and "you hit *you* with a hammer," but "he hit *himself* with a hammer." Notice here that the sentence "I hit me" is *not* ambiguous, whereas "he hit him" is ambiguous. The pronoun "me" cannot refer to anyone besides the speaker/writer, and similarly, the pronoun "you" cannot refer to anyone besides the audience/reader. Thus, in the first and second persons, one does not actually need reflexive pronouns, because the personal pronouns can serve unambiguously in their place. Thus, Latin is the most efficient here (as was older English), providing no more forms than are actually necessary. Greek and contemporary English provide "extra" forms ("myself" and "yourself" to go along with the essential "himself" and "herself").

Pointing Out or Emphasizing a Subject

In the dialogue between Nathan and Susan above, we saw that personal pronouns smoothed communication considerably. There are other types of pronouns that refer to persons or objects more remotely connected to the speaker/writer and listener/reader. Consider the following dialogue, with the pronouns underlined. Trey says, "I have been reading a great book this week, *War and Peace*." Ella responds, "Is *that* the one set in France during the Napoleonic Wars?" Trey answers, "No, *that* is *Les Misérables*. *This* is set during the Napoleonic Wars, but in Russia, not France." In this interchange, the words "this" and "that" point out two different books, one of which is near in the sense that it is the one Trey is reading now, and the other of which is more remote in that Trey and Ella know of it, but they are not reading it at the moment. "This" refers to the nearer book, and "that" refers to the more remote book.

These pronouns are called **demonstrative pronouns**, and as the name implies, they demonstrate or point out the subject. Greek has three demonstrative pronouns: οὗτος [houtos] ("this"), ἐκεῖνος [ekeinos] ("that"), and the rarer ὅδε [hode] ("this"). We have seen that because Latin does not have articles, it needs more pronouns, and in fact it has five demonstrative pronouns. Two of these are emphatic: *hic* ("*this* particular one") and *ille* ("*that* particular one"). Two are unemphatic: *is* and *iste,* both of which could be translated "that one." A fifth demonstrative pronoun is *idem* ("the same one"), and some grammarians consider *ipse* (also "the same one"), which I have mentioned above, to be a demonstrative pronoun rather than an intensive pronoun.

Referring to a Member of a Class

In some cases, one needs to use a pronoun to indicate not a specific subject, but any subject that falls into a certain class. In English, we say things such as "*Anyone* who wants to learn Latin must be dedicated to studying," or "*Someone* would need as much patience as intelligence to learn Greek." In these sentences, the pronouns "anyone" and "someone" do not refer to any particular person. Instead, they refer indefinitely to whoever might fulfill the qualifications the sentence gives—whoever might belong in the particular category of person the sentence describes. Thus, these are called **indefinite pronouns**. In Greek the indefinite pronoun is τις [tis], and in Latin it is *quis.* In keeping with the proliferation of pronouns in Latin, *quis* may be compounded to make similar pronouns such as *aliquis* ("anyone") and *quisquis* ("whoever").

Asking a Question

In many cases, one can ask a question using nouns and verbs, as in the example "Is Caroline home from school yet?" There are other questions, however, that virtually require pronouns. For example, suppose one wanted to ask not whether Caroline is home from school yet, but who is home from school at the moment. Obviously, one asks, "*Who* is home from school now?"

Could one ask this question without a pronoun like "who"? Well, one could ask, "Which person is home from school now?" This way of asking would substitute the adjective "which" and the noun "person" for the pronoun "who," but it would be more cumbersome. Or one could ask, "Is anyone home from school now?" This question would involve an indefinite pronoun and would not mean quite the same thing. Pronouns such as "who" are an important part of any Indo-European language, and they are called **interrogative pronouns** because they are used to ask questions. In Greek the interrogative pronoun is τίς [*tis*], and in Latin it is *quis*. Both of these words correspond to the English "who?" "whom?" or "what?" Notice that the forms of the interrogative pronouns are the same as those of the indefinite pronoun just above,[7] so the reader must recognize by context whether the pronoun introduces an indefinite reference to a subject or a question about a subject.

Linking a Subsequent Clause to a Previous Subject

As we have seen above, most pronouns refer to a previously mentioned subject. In those cases, the pronoun stands for that subject. In some cases, however, one needs to link an entire clause (not just a pronoun) back to a previous subject. For example, consider Paul's statement from 1 Corinthians 15:1: "I would remind you, brothers, of the gospel which I preached to you." In this sentence, the whole clause "which I preached to you" refers back to and explains the previous word, "gospel." This kind of clause is called a **relative clause**, because it "relates" to a previous subject. The pronoun used to introduce such a clause (in this case it is "which") is called a **relative pronoun**. The word to which the relative clause relates ("gospel," in this instance) is called the **antecedent**. The relative pronoun can be translated "who," "whom," "which," or "that" in English. In Greek there are two

7. In the case of Greek, this is an oversimplification. The interrogative pronoun and the indefinite pronoun are spelled the same way in all forms, but they differ in how they are accented. The indefinite pronoun is an enclitic, which means that its accent may be absent or may fall in an unexpected place in the word, depending on the words following it.

relative pronouns, ὅς [hos] and ὅστις [hostis]. In Latin, there is one, *qui*.

Pronoun Forms in Relation to the Words They Indicate

One of the important grammatical features related to pronouns is called **agreement**. In general, agreement means that words that are related to one another must possess comparable forms so as to indicate that relation. For example, we have already seen that adjectives must agree with the nouns they modify in gender, number, and case.[8] In Greek and Latin, pronouns must agree in gender and number with the words to which they refer. For example, if one were to use Greek or Latin to write the interchange between Trey and Ella about books, then when Trey says, "I am reading a great book," the word "book" would be in the accusative case, and in Greek it would be neuter singular, because the word for "book" is grammatically neuter, and in Latin masculine singular, because the word for "book" is grammatically masculine.

If Trey were to continue by saying, "I am reading a great book, which is set during the Napoleonic Wars," the word "which" would be a relative pronoun referring back to "book." So in Greek this pronoun would have to be neuter singular, and in Latin masculine singular. The pronoun would not be in the accusative case, however, because the case of the pronoun is determined by the way it is used in its own clause. "Which" is the subject of the relative clause "which is set during the Napoleonic Wars," even though its antecedent (the word to which it refers) is the object of the verb "am reading." So even though the pronoun agrees in gender and number with its antecedent, its case is determined by the way it is used in its own clause. If this is hard to grasp, consider that the sentence just above is approximately equivalent to saying, "I am reading a great book. This [book] is set during the Napoleonic Wars." When we write it as two separate sentences, it is clear that the pronoun "this" is the subject of its own sentence,

8. We shall see later that verbs must agree with their subjects in person and number: a plural subject requires a verb that is plural in form ("they swim," not "they swims.")

so it needs to be in the nominative case in Greek or Latin. In the sentence "I am reading a great book, which is set during the Napoleonic Wars," the relative pronoun "which" works exactly like the pronoun "this" in the statement, "I am reading a great book. This is set during the Napoleonic Wars."

This concept of agreement is crucial for understanding pronouns and the sentences in which they occur, so let me state the rule succinctly: *A pronoun must agree with its antecedent in gender and number, but it takes its case from its use in the clause/sentence of which it is a part.* Let us look at a more sophisticated biblical example. In 2 Timothy 2:8–9, Paul writes that Christ is descended from David, "as preached in my gospel, the gospel for which I am suffering and wearing fetters like a criminal." In this sentence, the clause "for which I am suffering" is a relative clause, and its antecedent is "gospel." In both Greek and Latin, "gospel" is neuter singular, and here it is accusative. Therefore, the relative pronoun "which" must be neuter and singular, but it cannot be accusative, because in its relative clause it functions as the object of the preposition translated "for," and that preposition takes the dative case in Greek and the ablative case in Latin. So the relative pronoun ᾧ [hōi] in Greek is neuter *dative* singular, and in Latin *quo* is neuter *ablative* singular, even though the antecedent of the pronoun is neuter *accusative* singular in either language.

As we conclude this chapter and this part of the book, let us look at a rather complicated example that illustrates how the Greek and Latin inflected forms help one in interpreting a text. In Romans 5:12, Paul asserts, "Therefore as sin came into the world through one man and death through sin, and so death spread to all men." What follows this assertion is a very controversial prepositional phrase, ἐφ' ᾧ [eph' hōi], translated "because" in the Revised Standard Version, and then the words "all men sinned." ἐφ' ᾧ [eph' hōi] means "corresponding to whom" or "corresponding to which." It is ambiguous because the word ᾧ [hōi] could be either masculine or neuter. (It is dative singular.) The question about this passage is, "What is the antecedent of the relative pronoun ᾧ [hōi]?" If ᾧ [hōi] is masculine, it could refer to Adam or to death, since obviously Adam is male, and the Greek word for death is grammatically masculine. If ᾧ [hōi] is neuter, it probably refers to the entire previous clause. So does death spread to all people, because "corresponding to Adam, all sinned" or because "corresponding to death, all sinned" or because "corresponding to the fact that sin and death have entered the world, all sinned"? Grammatically, one cannot tell which of these is the correct interpretation.

When one turns to the Latin Vulgate, the situation is slightly different. In Latin, the relative pronoun *quo* can still be masculine or neuter (it is ablative rather than dative), but in Latin, the word for "death" is feminine, so "death" cannot be the antecedent. Furthermore, the Vulgate interprets the strange preposition "corresponding to" to mean "in." So in Latin this text is stating that the reason death has passed to all men is that *in Adam* all sinned. Somehow, we were all present in Adam and took part in his sin. Notice that the differences between Greek and Latin have forced the translator of the Vulgate (Jerome) to decide whether the last clause was referring to Adam or to death. He could not retain the ambiguity that was there in Greek; the difference between Greek and Latin compelled him to resolve that ambiguity by interpreting the passage one way or another. The Vulgate may or may not be correct in its interpretation, but it is clearer than the Greek text. By reading the Vulgate, we today can recognize how the early Latin Church understood this crucial, but ambiguous passage. The Vulgate's translation of this passage has been extremely influential on the history of Western theology, and you now understand enough about Greek and Latin cases, nouns, and pronouns to grasp the way the Vulgate solidified a particular interpretation of an ambiguous text. Again, this is the sort of discovery that awaits you as you study the Bible and/or other texts in Greek or Latin (or better, in both languages).

As I have emphasized earlier, the system of cases in early Indo-European languages like Greek and Latin—a system that manifests itself in the forms of nouns, adjectives, articles (in Greek), and pronouns—may perhaps be the primary way these two languages differ from English. By now you should sufficiently understand how these cases work and the advantages they offer for communication, so you should be ready for the hard work of learning the case endings and the specific case usages as you study Greek or Latin. It is now time for us to turn our attention to verbs, which will be the subject of part 3 of this book.

APPENDIX: GRAMMATICAL TERMS INTRODUCED IN CHAPTER 5

Agreement: The grammatical concept that words that relate to one another must demonstrate their relation through similarity of form. Agreement can involve gender, number, case, and (in the case of verbs) person.

Antecedent: The word (usually a noun) to which a pronoun refers. The antecedent usually comes earlier in the sentence than the pronoun that refers to it.

Demonstrative pronoun: A pronoun that points out the subject to which it is referring.

Emphatic demonstrative pronoun: A pronoun that points out its subject while laying particular stress on that subject (e.g., "this particular one," "that particular one").

Indefinite pronoun: A pronoun that refers not to a particular subject, but to a subject as a member of a class (e.g., "anyone," "someone").

Intensive pronoun: A pronoun that gives great emphasis to the subject (e.g., "she *herself*").

Interrogative pronoun: A pronoun that is used in asking a question (e.g., "who?" "whom?" "what?").

Personal pronoun: A pronoun that refers either to the speaker/writer (first-person pronoun), the hearer/reader (second-person pronoun), or someone or something else (third-person pronoun) (e.g., "I," "you," "she"). Latin uses its demonstrative pronouns in place of a third-person pronoun.

Reflexive pronoun: A pronoun that refers back to the subject of the clause or sentence (e.g., "herself," "myself"). Latin uses its personal pronouns in place of reflexive pronouns in the first and second persons.

Relative clause: A clause that relates to a particular word (almost always a noun), usually earlier in a sentence.

Relative pronoun: A pronoun that governs a relative clause and refers back to a word (usually mentioned previously), called the **antecedent**.

Unemphatic demonstrative pronoun: A pronoun that points out its subject without laying particular stress on that subject (e.g., "that one").

PART 3   **VERBS: THE HEART OF COMMUNICATION**

6

WHAT DO VERBS DO?

My twelfth-grade English teacher was fond of telling her students that the strength of the English language lies in its verbs, and so great writing is built on the use of strong verbs, whereas poorer writing neglects its verbs and relies on piles of adjectives and adverbs to convey meaning and force. This is certainly true in English, but it is also true in any other Indo-European language. Verbs carry the weight when it comes to communicating; they drive the message that the sentence is trying to convey. If nouns formed the starting point for the grammatical part of this book, verbs constitute the heart of that grammatical discussion, and I will dedicate three chapters to verbs.

As we consider verbs, let us begin by asking about function. What exactly are verbs supposed to do? What should they accomplish in a sentence? We already know from chapter 3 that verbs express the central "event" of a sentence—the action or state the sentence is trying to convey. In this chapter I would like to introduce verbs by unpacking the many functions that are involved in conveying this central event, and then in the next two chapters, I will discuss the ways Greek and Latin verbs handle these tasks.

What Kinds of Events Must Verbs Describe?

Perhaps the most fundamental question related to verbs is what sorts of events are possible, and thus how verbs can describe the different kinds of events. Here there are two basic categories: an event can be either an action or a state. Some grammarians subdivide "action" into various other categories, because they see (for example) thought and speech as something different from action. Nevertheless, for most purposes it is sufficient simply to use these two categories. Either something is happening, or something is remaining in the state in which it already found itself. Either there is an action, or there is a state of being. Verbs that describe a state are sometimes called **stative verbs**. Verbs that describe an action are not automatically called active verbs, for reasons that I will make clear below.[1]

In the case of a verb that describes an action, another fundamental question is whether the action involves an object or is complete in itself. If a verb takes an object, it is said to be a **transitive verb**, because the action "carries over" to that object. (The word "transitive" comes from the Latin for "carry over.") If the action does not involve an object, the verb is said to be an **intransitive verb**. Some verbs, such as "to find," must always be transitive, because one has to have something to find, or the sentence does not make any sense. Other verbs, such as "to fare," must always be intransitive, since one cannot ask "to fare what?"; one can only ask whether a person is faring well or badly. Many verbs can be one or the other. For example, "to run" or "to swim" can be either transitive ("I am running a race" or "you are swimming laps") or intransitive ("I am going swimming today" or "she runs every day").

Who Is Doing the Action?

Another fundamental question is how the action or state is related to the subject of the sentence. If the verb is stative, then the subject of the sentence must be the one who is in that state. For example, if the "event" is being a teacher, then one can say, "I am a teacher," thus indicating that the subject ("I") is the one who is in that state. In contrast, if the verb describes an action, then in many cases the subject of the sentence can be either the one doing the action or the one receiving the action. For instance, instead of the stative event of being a teacher, consider the action of teaching. One can say, "I am teaching" or "the students are being taught." In the first case, the subject ("I") is performing

1. Instead, verbs that describe an action are called "fientive verbs," but you probably do not need to learn that term.

the action, and in the second case, the action is being performed on the subject ("the students"). They are receiving the action.

Grammatically, the question of whether the subject performs or receives the verb's action is called **voice**. You can remember this term by thinking of "voicing" an action as a synonym for "expressing" that action. How can we "voice" an action? How can we talk about it? We can voice the same action by saying either "I am teaching the students" or "the students are being taught by me." When the subject of the sentence performs the action indicated by the verb (or, for that matter, in the case of any stative verb where the subject is in that state), the verb is said to be in the **active voice**, and when the subject receives the action, the verb is said to be in the **passive voice**. Thus, a verb is not active just because it describes an action. If it describes an action, it can "voice" that action either actively or passively.

There is another possibility that I have not yet mentioned. If a verb describes an action, it is possible that the subject is performing the action on itself. For example, I could say, "I am teaching myself Greek." From our discussion of pronouns in the previous chapter, you can recognize "myself" as a reflexive pronoun, and you may want to say that this is "reflexive voice." In fact, there is no such grammatical category, although there certainly could be, since there is nothing sacrosanct about grammatical terminology. Even though there is no such term as "reflexive voice," the idea of the sentence above is clearly a reflexive one, and a language needs to be able to express such a reflexive idea. Latin and English express this reflexive idea the same way, by using a verb in the active voice ("am teaching") with a reflexive pronoun ("myself"). Greek can do this as well, since it has a reflexive pronoun, and obviously it has an active voice. Normally, however, Greek does not express the reflexive idea this way. Instead, it has another set of verb forms to use for reflexive action,[2]

2. Hebrew also possesses distinct verb forms for expressing reflexive action, and these are called Hithpael forms. One does not normally speak of active and passive voice in connection with Hebrew verbs, but if one were to do so, the Qal, Piel, and Hiphil forms would be considered active, the Niphal, Pual, and Hophal forms would be considered passive, and the Hithpael would be considered middle or reflexive.

and grammarians call these forms the **middle voice**. The middle voice is in between active and passive; that is, it describes a subject acting on itself rather than acting on another or being acted on by another. Once again, we see that there is more than one way to express a given idea, and Greek uses a different way than English most of the time, even though Greek has all the forms it needs to express reflexive action in the same way English does.[3]

Furthermore, the question of who is doing the action involves more than just specifying whether the subject performs the action, receives it, or acts on itself. This question also involves indicating how many people or things are included in the subject. As you know from our discussion of nouns, this is the question of number, and the possibilities are singular, plural, and (in the case of early Greek) dual. You know that nouns have separate forms for singular and plural in Greek and Latin, but so also do verbs. Just as English verbs can occasionally indicate how many subjects are performing the action ("she reads" vs. "they read"), so Latin and Greek verbs always indicate whether their subjects are singular or plural. In other words, there are separate forms for singular and plural verbs that you will have to learn. In early Greek there are also a few dual verb forms, but you will almost certainly not be asked to learn them. So for your purposes, a Greek or Latin verb form can be either **singular number** or **plural number**.

Finally, the question of who is doing the action requires that one relate the doer of the action to the speaker or writer of the sentence. Is the one who performs the action of the sentence the one who speaks/writes the sentence, the one who hears/reads the sentence, or another? From our study of pronouns, you know that these are called **first person** ("I" or "we"), **second person** ("you"), and **third person** ("he," "she," "it," or "they"). Like pronouns, Greek and Latin verbs have discrete forms to indicate whether the one doing the verb's action is first, second, or third person.

---

3. Students of Greek will be happy to know that in most cases, the forms for middle voice are the same as the forms for passive voice, so the presence of a middle voice in Greek does not give you many more forms to learn. Only the aorist and future tenses (which I will describe in the next chapter) have separate middle and passive forms.

Thus, from this question we can recognize that a verb needs to convey the **voice** of the action (active, middle, or passive), the **person** (first, second, or third), and the **number** (singular or plural). These are three of the pieces of information a Greek or Latin verb's form conveys, and in the next chapter I will discuss more fully how the forms are produced so as to convey this information.

What Is the Attitude toward the Action?

Another fundamental feature of a verb is the attitude that the subject takes toward that verb's action or state. Does the subject regard the action as something definite, as something hypothetical, as something she wishes would happen, as something that needs to happen, or as something that has not happened or will not happen? Recognize that the subject of the action may have a definite attitude toward the action, but the speaker/writer may know that the subject is wrong. Ideally, a language's verbs should be able to indicate this kind of subtlety, as well, although many languages have trouble with this. For example, take the following assertion: "The teacher failed the student because he cheated." Focus here on the student's action of cheating. From the point of view of the teacher, that action was definite: the student really cheated. Was the teacher right, though? Perhaps the teacher was mistaken, or the student was framed, or something of that sort. The clause "because he cheated" does not actually address the issue of whether the action that the teacher thought happened really did happen, but if one had to guess, one would have to say that the sentence, as written, implies that the student really did cheat. Now consider another way to cast this sentence: "The teacher failed the student on the grounds that he cheated." Here the switch from "because" to "on the grounds that" casts some doubt on whether the student really cheated. Once again, from the teacher's point of view, the action actually happened, but this time the speaker/writer is not so sure that the teacher is right, and the sentence reflects some doubt about whether the cheating really took place.

This issue of the attitude toward the action or state is called **mood** in grammatical terminology. Mood is one of the most complex elements of Indo-European verbs, and I will discuss it in more detail in the next chapter. For now, it is sufficient to state that originally in Indo-European languages there were four basic moods of verbs, which I will introduce briefly here.

Indicative Mood. This is the mood for making a basic affirmation or declaration, for indicating an event. It assumes factuality—from the point of view of the subject, the event really happens. Or, in the case of a question, the point is to ask whether the event is really happening. For example, one may say, "Lauren is a great Latin teacher," or one may ask, "Is Lauren a great Latin teacher?" In both cases the verb "is" goes in the indicative mood.

Imperative Mood. This is the mood for giving a command, as its name indicates. In the sentence "Brush your teeth before bedtime," the verb is in the imperative mood. I should note here that in most languages there are other ways to give a command (like saying, "You must brush your teeth before bedtime"), but the imperative mood is the most basic way to do so. In Latin, like in English, there are imperative forms only for the second person (singular and plural), since in these languages the imperative idea implies that the one (or ones) whom a person is commanding is (or are) also the one (or ones) to whom that person is talking or writing. In Greek, however, there are also third-person imperatives, which translate into English as "let her do this" or "let them do this." If one wants to give a command in the third person in Latin, or in the first person in Greek or Latin ("let me do this") or ("let us do this"), one uses the subjunctive mood instead of the imperative.

Subjunctive and Optative Moods. These moods are for expressing actions that are possible, hypothetical, or doubtful. In languages that still possess an optative mood (like Greek, although it occurs rarely in the New Testament—only about seventy times total), the optative is more remote than the subjunctive. So if one wanted to say, "I hope I do well on the exam," then "do" might call for a subjunctive construction, but if one wanted to say, "I wish I would do well on the exam," then "would do" might call for an optative construction. So with a subjunctive and an optative, a language can express fine shades of meaning, from certainty, to hopefulness, to wishful thinking. If a language possesses only a subjunctive but not an optative (as Latin and English do—although English is rapidly losing even its subjunctive now), then it has to use the subjunctive in various different constructions to handle everything less than certainty.

Here we see that in any language whose verb system is sophisticated enough, there should be a way to indicate whether an action has happened (or will happen), whether it must or ought to happen, or whether it is doubtful whether it has happened or will happen, or even whether it cannot have happened or cannot happen. These questions of attitude are handled in Greek and Latin by forms for the **moods** and various specific uses of these moods.

At What Time Does the Action Take Place?

At first glance, this seems like a very simple question. An action can take place (or a state can exist) in the **past**, the **present**, or the **future**. Of course, this simple answer is correct, but we need to remember that just as one must consider both the subject's and the speaker's/writer's attitude toward the action, so one must consider time in relation to both the subject and the speaker/writer. Consider the following sentence: "It is raining." This is obviously a reference to the present time. Now imagine a speaker talking about the event of rain: "Glenn says that it is raining." Both verbs still refer to present time. Now put the action of speaking in the past: "Glenn said that it was raining." This sentence means that it was raining at the time he spoke, but one could also write, "Glenn said that it had been raining" or "Glenn said that it would be raining." In the first case, his action of speaking was in the past, and the rain came prior to that past speaking. In the second case, his action of speaking was in the past, and the rain was going to come subsequent to his speaking. You can see here that very quickly the fine shades of meaning with respect to time start to multiply as the sentence becomes more complex. You should recognize as well that different languages relate the time of the main action (Glenn's speaking) to the time of the action in the subordinate clause (the rain) in different ways. Some languages leave the forms of the subordinate verb the same as they would be if the action of speaking were still in the present. So to say "Glenn said that it will be raining" would, in some languages, be the equivalent of what we would express in English as "Glenn said that it would be raining." The issue of how one relates the **time** of the various verbs in a sentence is called **sequence** or **consecution**. These terms are interchangeable, and you can remember the second if you associate it with the word "consecutive." Sequence or consecution of verbs in Greek and Latin is one of the major things you will need to learn toward the end of your first year of study, and I will return to this issue in the next chapter.

What Type of Action Is Being Described?

This is the last of our introductory questions about verbs, and it has to do with whether the action of a given verb is ongoing, completed, or viewed as a whole without specifying whether it is ongoing or not. Consider the following sentences: "Fred swam laps yesterday." "Fred used to swim laps every day." "Fred was swimming laps when a storm rolled in, and he had to leave the pool." In the first of these sentences, the verb "swam" probably refers to a completed action (Fred set out to swim a certain number of laps, and he finished them), although one could understand it as referring to an action considered as a whole, without regard to whether that action was completed or not. The second sentence refers to a habitual action in the past, an ongoing action, rather than a completed one. In the third sentence, the verb for swimming refers to an action that was in process (and therefore not completed) at the time another action happened.

The question of whether an action is ongoing, completed, or viewed as a whole (unspecified) is called **aspect**. A verb describing ongoing action is said to have **imperfect aspect** or **progressive aspect**. A verb describing a completed action is said to have **perfect aspect**, and a verb describing an action as a whole, with no reference to whether it is completed or not, is said to have **simple** or **indefinite aspect**. In the next chapter, I will consider the way Greek, Latin, and English handle the question of aspect.

It is probably important for you to know these terms for aspect, but for reasons that will become apparent in the next chapter, I will not use them. Instead, I will use nontechnical words to describe aspect: ongoing, completed, and unspecified.

One of the words you will hear very often as you study Greek or Latin is **tense**. Many students, and even some grammarians, regard "tense" as a synonym for time. For reasons that will become apparent in the next chapter, I think it is more helpful to think of tense as a combination of time and aspect. As you learn a classical language, you will study the forms for the various tenses (six of them in Latin, seven in Greek, although you may learn only five or six of those seven). You should understand each of these tenses as indicating a certain time and a certain aspect, rather than thinking of them as simply indicating time. Because this is the point at which I think it is most harmful to refer students back to English, I am not going to discuss or name the English tenses. Instead, I will deal in the next chapter with the various combinations of time and aspect that lead to the Greek and Latin verb tenses. At that point, I hope to convince you that Greek and Latin are elegant in handling this combination. For now, though, it is sufficient simply to recognize that a verb has to indicate both time and aspect, and the combination of these two (for example, past time and ongoing aspect—"Fred was swimming") is called tense.

Putting the Pieces Together

Thus, a typical verb in Greek or Latin conveys quite a lot of information about the event it describes. Table 6-1 (page 112) summarizes what we have covered in this chapter.

Just as you will learn to recognize a given noun or adjective form as indicating a certain gender, number, and case, so you will learn to identify a given verb form in terms of these questions and their possible answers. Be aware, however, that this chart does not yet contain all of the "correct" answers to the questions of form identification. Rather than identifying a given form as indicating a certain time and a certain aspect, you will learn that it indicates a certain tense, and you will understand that

Table 6-1 Verb Function in Greek and Latin

Question	Grammatical Term	Possible Answers in Greek/Latin
What is the attitude toward the action?	Mood	Indicative, Imperative, Subjunctive, Optative (Greek only)
Does the subject perform or receive the action?	Voice	Active, Middle (Greek only), Passive
How is the subject related to the speaker/writer?	Person	First, Second, Third
How many subjects are there?	Number	Singular, Dual (Greek only), Plural
When does the action occur?	[Time]	Present, Past, Future
What kind of action is described?	[Aspect]	Completed, Ongoing, Unspecified

tense as combination of time and aspect. So the last two questions in this table will be combined into one as soon as we have considered verb tenses in the next chapter. Nevertheless, even as it stands now, this table gives you a clear idea of what a given verb form needs to convey and how a Greek or Latin verb does so.

Any verb in Greek or Latin that exhibits all of these characteristics (that is, a verb that can be described in terms of mood, voice, tense, person, and number) is called a **finite verb form**. Of course, the word "finite" means "limited," and grammatically, a finite verb form is one whose use is limited by its form. It must apply to a certain subject (person and number), it must convey a certain type of action at a certain time, and with a certain attitude (mood), because it is in a form that demands that it do so. Technically, it is the limitation to a particular person and mood that makes a verb finite, as we shall see in the next two chapters. Verbal forms that are not considered finite still communicate a certain tense, voice, and often number, but not mood or person.

In chapter 3, I wrote that a clause is a group of words that includes a subject and a predicate and expresses a complete idea. At that point, I wrote that one cannot actually understand a clause until one grasps the concept of a finite verb. Now that we have covered that concept, we are in a better position to understand the difference between a phrase and a clause. A verbal phrase includes a non-finite verbal form such as an infinitive or a participle. In contrast, a clause includes a finite verb form (or, in the case of a clause without a verb, it contains an implied finite verb form). To illustrate this difference again, let us go back to one of the first examples from chapter 1: "I want you to do this for me." In this sentence, "you to do this for me" is often called an infinitive clause in English, because it includes a subject "you" and a verb "to do." If you were to express this idea this way in Greek or Latin (which you would not normally do), then the equivalent of "you to do this for me" would be an infinitive phrase because it contains a non-finite verbal form rather than a finite verb. If you were to say the sentence the way you should say it in Greek or Latin—the equivalent of "I want that you do this for me"—then "that you do for me" is a clause because the verb form would be a finite verb with a particular person (second) and a particular mood (subjunctive). In Greek and Latin, unlike in English, the key to a clause is a finite verb (stated or implied).

In the next chapter, I will consider finite verb forms in Greek and Latin by focusing in more detail on tense and mood. (Person, number, and voice should be clear from my brief discussions in this chapter.) Then in chapter 8, I will introduce the **non-finite verb forms** in Greek and Latin—that is, infinitives and participles.[4]

APPENDIX: GRAMMATICAL TERMS INTRODUCED IN CHAPTER 6

Active voice: A grammatical category for expressing action in which the subject is the one performing that action.

Aspect: An indication of whether the action is ongoing, completed, or not specified.

---

4. Latin also has gerunds and gerundives, which I will consider in connection with participles.

Consecution: The way a given language relates verbs to one another within a complex sentence. Consecution can involve relations between verb tenses and/or relations between verb moods. Another word for consecution is **sequence**.

Finite verb form: A verb form that is limited to a particular person. A finite verb form will also possess mood.

First-person verb: A verb form that indicates that the subject of the event is the speaker/writer of the sentence.

Future time: Time subsequent to the present.

Imperative mood: A grammatical category for giving a command or making a prohibition.

Imperfect aspect: A grammatical category for indicating that the action of the verb is ongoing, progressive, or incomplete at the time the sentence takes place.

Indefinite aspect: A grammatical category for indicating that the sentence does not specify whether the action is ongoing or completed.

Indicative mood: A grammatical category for indicating that an event is taking place, was taking place, or will take place, or for asking a question about an event.

Intransitive verb: A verb that does not need an object to complete its meaning.

Middle voice: In Greek, a grammatical category for indicating that the subject is performing the action on itself. Latin does not have a middle voice.

Mood: A grammatical category for expressing the attitude of the subject and/or the speaker/writer to the event of the sentence.

Non-finite verb form: A verb form that is not limited to a particular person and therefore does not possess mood.

Optative mood: In Greek, a grammatical category for indicating events that are very uncertain, events that one hopes or wishes might happen.

Passive voice: A grammatical category for indicating that the subject is receiving the verb's action, not performing that action.

Past time: Time prior to the present.

Perfect aspect: A grammatical category for indicating that the action of the verb has already been completed at the time the sentence takes place.

Person: A grammatical concept that indicates whether the subject is the speaker/writer of the sentence, the hearer/reader, or someone else.

Present time: The time when the sentence takes place.

Second-person verb: A verb form that indicates that the subject of the event is the hearer/reader of the sentence.

Sequence: The way a given language relates verbs to one another within a complex sentence. Sequence can involve relations between verb tenses and/or relations between verb moods. Another word for sequence is **consecution**.

Simple aspect: A grammatical category for speaking/writing of an action as a whole, without indicating whether it is completed or ongoing.

Stative verb: A verb that conveys a state of being, rather than an action.

Subjunctive mood: A grammatical category for indicating events that are less than certain.

Tense: A grammatical category that combines time and aspect; thus, a way of indicating both when an action takes place and whether it is ongoing, completed, or unspecified.

Third-person verb: A verb form that indicates that the subject of the event is someone other than the speaker/writer or the hearer/reader.

Time: An indication of when the event takes place—in the past, the present, or the future.

Transitive verb: A verb that needs an object to complete its meaning.

Voice: A grammatical category for indicating whether the subject performs or receives the action of the sentence.

7

FINITE VERB FORMS

A Closer Look at Tense and Mood

In the previous chapter, we considered five major questions that verbs answer about the event (action or state) that the clause or sentence describes. From these five questions, we eventually arrived at the grammatical categories of voice, person, number, mood, and tense.[1] Of these five, the ones that are most complicated, and the ones on which Latin and Greek diverge the most from English, are tense and mood. Accordingly, in this chapter I will examine these categories in some detail.

Tense: The Interplay of Time and Aspect

As I mentioned in the previous chapter, "tense" is not a synonym for time. Rather it is a technical term for the identifiably distinct forms of verbs. The "tenses" of Greek and Latin verbs convey something about the time and the aspect of a given action. This is true in English as well, but not in the same way. Because the classical tenses do not correspond closely to the tenses of English verbs, it is better not even to name the English tenses at all in discussions of Greek or Latin verbs. There is little point in studying a tense in English that does not correspond well to a Greek or Latin tense, and even if the tense corresponds reasonably well, the tense's name may not correspond. Accordingly, in this sec-

1. Notice that it was not the case that each question led to one category in a one-to-one correspondence. Rather, the five categories were the end product of a line of reasoning that involved five sequential questions.

tion I would like to discuss the ways time and aspect relate in general in any Indo-European language,[2] and then specifically the ways Greek and Latin verb tenses handle time and aspect. In the process, I will give English *translations* for the ideas of the various tenses, but I will not name English *tenses*, because doing so, in my opinion, simply creates confusion.[3]

Let us consider what we learned about time and aspect in the previous chapter. Obviously, the time of an action can be past, present, or future. Furthermore, the aspect of an action can be completed (called "perfect"), ongoing (called "imperfect" or "progressive"), or unspecified. (In the third case, the action is viewed as a whole without reference to its aspect. Aspect that is not specified is usually called "indefinite" or "simple.") If we put time and aspect together into the various possible combinations, we come up with something like table 7-1 (page 118). Notice that in this table and throughout this section, I use nontechnical words such as "ongoing," "completed," and "unspecified" to describe aspect, rather than using the technical linguistic terms "imperfect," "perfect," and "indefinite." By doing this, I hope to help you avoid confusing the aspect names with the tense names that I will introduce shortly, some of which include the words "perfect" and "imperfect."

From this table we can see that an ideal Indo-European language might have nine tenses—nine different combinations of time and aspect. In fact, English has even more—twelve different tenses, the way many grammarians classify them. Here,

2. It is worth noting here that non-Indo-European verbs often bear very little similarity to Indo-European verbs on these points. For example, Hebrew verbs, considered in themselves, have little time referent at all. They primarily indicate aspect, and one must normally use the context to determine the time of the action.

3. Notice that to some degree, this is what I have done all along. When I introduced the case system, I discussed the three English cases only to show you that the idea of cases is not completely foreign to you. I did not draw any connections between Greek/Latin cases and English cases, nor did I argue that certain cases in the classical languages worked like certain English cases. Instead, I explained cases on their own, with illustrations of how to translate them into English, but not with reference to English grammatical categories. What I am about to do in the case of verb tenses is another example of the pattern I have tried to follow throughout the book.

Table 7-1 Time and Aspect in Indo-European Verbs

	Ongoing Aspect	Completed Aspect	Unspecified Aspect
Past Time	Action that was ongoing at a given point in the past ("I was doing")	Action that, at a given point in the past, had been completed ("I had done")	Action that pertains to the past ("I did")
Present Time	Action that is ongoing at the present moment ("I am doing")	Action that, at the present moment, has been completed ("I have done")	Action that pertains to the present ("I do")
Future Time	Action that will be ongoing at a given point in the future ("I will be doing")	Action that, at a given point in the future, will have been completed ("I will have done")	Action that pertains to the future ("I will do")

though, one should consider an important difference between English, on one hand, and Greek or Latin, on the other. In English, there are only four basic forms for each verb, as you can see from the words "do," "doing," "did," and "done" in table 7-1. The forms for conveying the various time-aspect relations are achieved primarily by adding helping verbs like "will," "was," "have," and "will have" to the four basic forms. Languages like English, French, and German build their verbs from a main word and various helping verbs; in contrast, Greek and Latin verbs usually consist of only one word, and never more than two words. The verb forms have to be built up by changes within the basic word, not normally by adding other words to the basic word. Because changes within a word are more complicated than external changes, there was a tendency in the early development of Greek and Latin to eliminate unnecessary forms, to have no more tenses than were actually required.

In light of that tendency, take another look at the table above. In future time, the distinction between unspecified aspect and ongoing aspect is virtually nonexistent. In English we can say "I will be doing," but do we say this? Rarely. In most cases, simply saying "I will do" is quite sufficient.[4] Having separate forms for future unspecified action and future ongoing action is really introducing more complexity than a verb system needs. Similarly, the distinction between unspecified aspect and ongoing aspect in the present time is not really needed, either. In English we make such a distinction ("I do" is not quite the same thing as "I am doing"), but most languages do very well without this fine distinction. If an action is happening in the present, it is by definition ongoing. So having separate tenses for present unspecified action and present ongoing action also introduces needless complexity. Furthermore, recognize that if, at the present time, an action has been completed, that means that it was completed in the past at some point, so one could also argue that distinguishing past unspecified action and present completed action is unnecessary.

If one were to think in this way, then one could conceive of a verb system in terms of only two aspects (completed and ongoing), with no distinctions of forms for unspecified aspect. In such a case, writers and speakers could use the context to indicate unspecified aspect, but the forms would indicate only completed or ongoing action. This is exactly what Latin does, and one can argue that Latin verb tenses are as simple and elegant as possible. The language has all the tenses one really needs, but unlike English it possesses no unneeded tenses to complicate matters. Table 7-2 (page 120) indicates the basic scheme for Latin verb tenses, considered in terms of two aspects, and includes the names of those tenses. Compare this table carefully to table 7-1 and reread the intervening paragraphs to understand how one goes from the theoretical nine tenses an Indo-European language might have to the six tenses Latin actually possesses.

An important implication of this verb scheme is that in Latin, verb tenses are primarily a matter of time, with less consideration of aspect. Thus, for example, Latin has no distinction of

4. In fact, in English we often forgo future forms altogether in favor of present forms, even when the action pertains to the future. For example, instead of saying, "When I will have arrived, I will see you," we say, "When I arrive, I will see you." Since we possess these complicated future forms but rarely use them, we should be able to imagine a language that can get by without as many future forms as we have in English.

Table 7-2 Latin Verbs Considered in Terms of Two Aspects

	Ongoing Action	*Completed Action*
Past	Action that was ongoing at a given point in the past ("I was doing") *Imperfect Tense*	Action that, at a given point in the past, was already completed ("I had done") *Pluperfect Tense* Action that took place in the past ("I did," "I have done") *Perfect Tense*
Present	Action that is ongoing at the present moment ("I am doing," "I do") *Present Tense*	——
Future	Action that will be ongoing at a given point in the future ("I will be doing," "I will do") *Future Tense*	Action that, at a given point in the future, will have been completed ("I will have done") *Future Perfect Tense*

form to convey the aspect difference between an action done in the past viewed from the simple fact that it was done ("I did"), and an action done in the past viewed from the point of view that it is completed now ("I have done"), although Latin can indicate such a distinction of aspect by the context of the sentence. Focusing on time more than aspect enables Latin to function with fewer verb tenses, while still giving it enough forms to handle the situations that arise.

In Greek, the situation is slightly more complicated than in Latin, but still simpler than in English. If one wants to think in terms of two aspects (completed and ongoing), then the one difference between Greek and Latin is that Greek does make a distinction in form between an action done in the past viewed from the simple fact that it was done ("I did"), and an action done in the past viewed from the point of view that it is completed now ("I

Table 7-3 Greek Verbs Considered in Terms of Two Aspects

	Ongoing Action	Completed Action
Past	Action that was ongoing at a given point in the past ("I was doing") *Imperfect Tense*	Action that, at a given point in the past, was already completed ("I had done") *Pluperfect Tense* Action that took place in the past ("I did," "I have done") *Aorist Tense*
Present	Action that is ongoing at the present moment ("I am doing," "I do") *Present Tense*	Action that, at the present moment, has already been completed ("I have done") *Perfect Tense*
Future	Action that will be ongoing at a given point in the future ("I will be doing," "I will do") *Future Tense*	Action that, at a given point in the future, will have been completed ("I will have done") *Future Perfect Tense*

have done"). This gives Greek seven tenses, as shown in table 7-3.

Table 7-3 is probably sufficient for you, a beginning Greek student, to reflect on time and aspect, but grammarians agree that Greek verbs are more focused on aspect than Latin verbs are. So from a linguistic point of view, table 7-4 (page 122), in which distinctions among three aspects are preserved, is more technically accurate to describe Greek.

In later Greek, such as that of the New Testament, the pluperfect tense is rare,[5] and the future perfect is even rarer.[6] Be-

5. This is because the idea of the pluperfect—action that had already been completed at the time another past action was taking place—is easily handled in Greek by a different construction, an aorist participle (which I will discuss in the next chapter).

6. This is because the distinction between completed and ongoing action is not normally crucial when the action is in the future. If it has not happened yet, why does one need to specify whether it will be ongoing or continuous?

Table 7-4 Greek Verbs Considered in Terms of Three Aspects

	Ongoing Action	*Completed Action*	*Unspecified Aspect*
Past	Action that was ongoing at a given point in the past ("I was doing") *Imperfect Tense*	Action that, at a given point in the past, was already completed ("I had done") *Pluperfect Tense*	Action that pertains to the past ("I did") *Aorist Tense*
Present	Action that is ongoing at the present moment ("I am doing," "I do") *Present Tense*	Action that, at the present moment, has already been completed ("I have done") *Perfect Tense*	———
Future	Action that will be ongoing at a given point in the future ("I will be doing," "I will do") *Future Tense*	Action that, at a given point in the future, will have been completed ("I will have done") *Future Perfect Tense*	———

Table 7-5 Verbs in Later Greek, Considered in Terms of Three Aspects

	Ongoing Action	*Completed Action*	*Unspecified Aspect*
Past	Action that was ongoing at a given point in the past ("I was doing") *Imperfect Tense*	Action that, at a given point in the past, was already completed ("I had done") *Pluperfect Tense* [RARE]	Action that pertains to the past ("I did") *Aorist Tense*
Present	Action that is ongoing at the present moment ("I am doing," "I do") *Present Tense*	Action that, at the present moment, has already been completed ("I have done") *Perfect Tense*	———
Future	———	———	Action that will take place in the future ("I will be doing," "I will do") *Future Tense*

Table 7-6 Verb Tenses in Greek and Latin

Greek Tense Name	Time of Action	Aspect of Action	Latin Tense Name
Present	Present	Ongoing	Present
Imperfect	Past	Ongoing	Imperfect
Future	Future	Ongoing (or unspecified)	Future
Aorist	Past	Unspecified (or completed)	Perfect
Perfect	Past/Present	Completed but with continuing results	Perfect
Pluperfect	Past	Completed	Pluperfect
Future Perfect	Future	Completed	Future Perfect

cause the future perfect tense is so rare, the distinction between ongoing and completed action in the future is basically lost, and one may think of the future tense as conveying action with unspecified aspect. In this case, the interplay of tense and aspect follows table 7-5.

Thus, we see that whether one thinks in terms of two aspects (as is usually sufficient in Latin) or three (as is necessary in Greek to understand the aorist tense), Greek and Latin both have simpler verb tense systems than English does. This is why it is easier to understand these tenses on their own terms than it is to understand them with reference to the more complicated English tenses. Table 7-6 summarizes much of the material I have covered in this section, in a way that may help you to remember the information more easily. Notice that the greater attention to aspect in Greek means that it has two tenses (aorist and perfect) that do the work of one tense (perfect) in Latin. Notice also that unlike tables 7-1 through 7-5, table 7-6 does not go from past to present to future time, but is recast into the order in which you will likely learn the tenses. As a result, table 7-6 is probably the one to which you will want to refer as you learn the Greek or Latin verb system.

From Time to Aspect to Mood

In the previous chapter's introduction to verbs, I briefly discussed four moods: indicative, imperative, subjunctive, and optative. At that point I was not yet able to give a fuller discussion of these moods, because in the classical languages mood and tense are so closely related that they can scarcely be understood separately. Now that I have discussed tense in a bit more detail, we are ready to return to mood and to round out our understanding of it. I would like to divide this section into three subsections: the relation between tense and mood, the function of mood in independent clauses, and the function of mood in subordinate clauses.

The Relation between Tense and Mood: From Simplicity to Complexity and Back

Consider the following sentence, as a sportscaster giving a post-game highlight show talks about a crucial play during that day's football game: "If he makes that block, they win the game." You can probably recognize that this is not particularly good English, but why not? In this sentence, both verbs are in the present, but the event being described has already happened. Why does the sportscaster speak in the present about an event in the past? Doing so adds immediacy; it makes the audience feel as if the event is happening right now, but notice that the verbs of this sentence are not at all equivalent. The first one refers to an event that did not happen (the player did not successfully make the block), and the other one refers to an event that did not happen either, but it *would have* happened if the first event had happened. Of course, it would be better English for the sportscaster to say, "If he *had made* that block, they *would have won* the game." This is the correct way in English to refer to an event in the past that was contrary to fact (it could have happened but did not) and an event also in the past that was conditioned upon that first event (it would have happened if that first event had happened, but the first event did not happen, so the second event did not happen, either). Notice that this sentence expresses a rather complex thought, and it does so using only present indicative verbs, because in context the listeners know that the event being described did not happen. It is not good English, but in context it is clear. It communicates well, and one hears sentences like this quite often (not just from athletes or sportscasters). Consider another sentence, though. A mother says to her daughter, "I wished you will become a teacher." This is obviously not good English either, and unlike the previous example, this is probably not something you ever hear from a native English speaker (although I have heard native Spanish speakers say something like this in English). Even though this is not good English, it still communicates reasonably well: the mother wanted her daughter to become a teacher, but that did not happen.

Why do I give these examples? What do they have in common? In both cases, an event that is doubtful or contrary to fact is being expressed by using language that refers to a time period subsequent to when the event really happened. The sportscaster uses the present tense to refer to an event in the past that could have happened but that did not actually happen, and the mother uses the future tense to refer to the same thing, a possible event in the past that did not happen. To use linguistic terminology, both sentences describe contrary-to-fact situations (for which one should use the subjunctive mood in English) by using the indicative mood and a tense subsequent to the tense they should have been using. Ironically, the increasingly rapid loss of the subjunctive in English is being counteracted by using verb tenses to do the work of verb moods. The resulting speech is not elegant—at least not to purists—but sentences like the ones in these examples do communicate well enough.

Ironically, the use of tenses to do the work of moods constitutes a return of language to its origins. In the pre-literary period of the Indo-European languages, people probably expressed wishes, doubts, and the like using tenses (especially the future tense), not moods. Linguists believe that the various moods arose out of the tenses, and during the heyday of the Indo-European languages (the age of classical Sanskrit, Greek, and Latin), the forms and uses of the various moods were quite complex. Nevertheless, the moods never lost their dependence on tense, and as the languages continue to devolve today, the use of the moods is gradually being replaced by the use of tense to convey the speaker's attitude toward the action. In this case, the languages are coming full circle.

With respect to Greek and Latin, this history lesson should remind us that mood and tense are not unrelated categories. Mood is affected by tense, because it grows out of tense. More specifically, mood is an extension of the aspect element in tense. How one looks at a given action (as opposed to when it occurs)— which grammatically is called aspect—is the steppingstone to mood or the attitude of the speaker/writer toward the action. For your purposes, this means that in moods other than the indicative, the aspect element of tense is more prominent and the time aspect of tense is less prominent. For you to understand how this will play out in the forms you will have to learn, let us consider the implications of this for each of the moods.

The indicative, of course, is the basic mood of speech and writing. We have already seen that in Latin the tenses of the indicative are more time-oriented than they are aspect-oriented, whereas in Greek the indicative tenses are more aspect-oriented and a bit less time-oriented. (Remember that in both languages, tenses convey both time and aspect. The difference is one of degree.) When one moves from the indicative to the imperative, verbs lose virtually all of their time reference. After all, one cannot very well give a command about the past! Commands by definition refer to the present or the near future. So in Latin, like in English, there are essentially no discrete tenses of the imperative mood. There is simply the attitude of urgency—"do this!"[7]— so we speak of imperatives as "present tense." Because Greek tenses convey more aspect than Latin or English tenses do, Greek does preserve three different tenses in the imperative mood: the present, the perfect, and the aorist. They have no time reference, but they do convey the aspect of the various tenses. So in Greek a present imperative conveys the idea of continuing to do what one is already doing (the ongoing aspect of the present tense), an aorist imperative focuses on the action itself and urges

7. Again, this is a slight oversimplification. Latin verbs originally had future imperatives as well, and a few verbs (such as "to be") continued to exhibit these forms in classical and Christian Latin literature. There is scarcely any difference in function between future and present imperatives.

the hearer/reader simply to do that (the unspecified aspect of the aorist tense), and a perfect imperative focuses on retaining the effects of a past action (again, the nuance grows out of the aspect reference of the perfect tense). The last of these is especially difficult for an English speaker to grasp, but consider Jesus' command to the wind and the sea in Mark 4:39, "Peace! Be still!" In Greek the word for "be still" is a perfect imperative (πεφίμωσο [pephimōso]), which more literally means "keep the muzzle on." The idea is that the sea has been muzzled (that is, that Christ has already gained control over it), and he is commanding the effects of that muzzling to remain and to become manifest. In contrast to the great specificity of the Greek imperative, Latin and English must resort to present imperatives (basically the only kind we have) to approximate the force of what Jesus says here. The greater focus on aspect in Greek verb tenses enables it to retain different tenses in the imperative, and so to gain nuances of the imperative that Latin and English do not have.

Similarly, in the subjunctive and optative, the time referent is vastly reduced in comparison with the indicative. Because of this, Greek and Latin have fewer tenses in these moods than in the indicative (although more than they have in the imperative). In the subjunctive, Latin has four tenses (present, imperfect, perfect, and pluperfect), and these tenses indicate primarily the type of action (ongoing action in the case of present or imperfect; completed action in the case of perfect or pluperfect). Greek has three subjunctive tenses (present, aorist, and perfect) and four optative tenses (present, future, aorist, and perfect), but it rarely uses its future or perfect optative or its perfect subjunctive. Much more common are the present (indicating ongoing action) and the aorist (indicating completed action), with no time element involved. Remember again that koine Greek rarely uses its optative at all. It uses the subjunctive in places where earlier Greek would use the optative, and thus it functions more like Latin.

For your purposes now, the important thing to remember is that mood affects the balance between time and aspect within a given tense. When one moves out of the indicative mood to the imperative, subjunctive, or optative, the time element implied in a given tense is vastly reduced, if not eliminated, and one is left essentially with the aspect element conveyed by that tense. Thus, fewer tenses are needed in these nonindicative moods than in the indicative.

Mood in Independent Clauses

It should be apparent that the imperative mood is used exclusively in independent clauses, since, after all, a command can always be a sentence in and of itself, and thus it constitutes an independent clause by itself. The presence of a command makes a clause independent. It should also be clear by now how imperatives are used. Remember also that Greek and Latin can use the subjunctive in an independent clause to take the place of an imperative. As we have seen, Greek possesses second- and third-person imperative forms, but Latin (like English) has only second-person imperatives. To take the place of missing imperative forms (such as "let her do this" in Latin or "let us do this" in either language), the subjunctive is used with an imperative sort of force.[8]

In addition to their use in place of an imperative, the subjunctive and optative can also be used in an independent clause to refer to a possible event in the future. In fact, this is the sort of construction in which these two moods originally arose, and this is where the subjunctive and optative show most clearly the characteristics I discussed when I introduced them in the previous chapter. That is, in independent clauses, these two moods are used to refer to future possibilities, and the Greek indicative indicates an event that will certainly happen, the subjunctive a probable or possible event, and the optative a more remotely possible event. Since Latin has no optative, the indicative indicates a certain event, and the subjunctive a possible event, with no grammatical distinction between likely and unlikely. Consider these closely related sentences: "You will see your grandchildren

8. Grammatically, using a subjunctive with imperative force in the first person ("let us do this") is called "hortatory subjunctive," and using a subjunctive in the third person ("let her do this") is called "jussive subjunctive." These are terms you may not need to learn.

and their children." "May you see your grandchildren and their children." "Might you see your grandchildren and their children." All of these sentences are referring to a possible event in the future: the addressee's living long enough to see her second- and third-generation descendants. The first sentence regards that event as certain, and so if one were saying this in Greek or Latin, the verb for "will see" would go in the future indicative. The second sentence regards that event as possible and expresses the hope that it may happen, but it does not see the event as nearly so certain. In Greek or Latin, the verb for "may see" would go in the present subjunctive. One could argue that in English, the third sentence is no different from the second, but it is possible to discern here that the speaker regards the possibility of the addressee's living to see her descendants to be more remote than in the second case. Latin cannot very well handle the distinction between the second and third sentences, but Greek is able to make such a fine distinction by using the future optative in the third sentence. Remember that in chapter 2, I mentioned that Greek is better than Latin at expressing fine nuances and shades of meaning, and the presence of both an optative and a subjunctive in Greek is part of the reason for this.

An appropriate example of the use of the Greek optative in an independent clause is Paul's famous exclamation μὴ γένοιτο [mē genoito], which occurs fifteen times in the New Testament (out of seventy total uses of the optative). This is a negative optative, and so it constitutes an attempt to remove all possibility of a given action from view. (It is translated "By no means!" in the Revised Standard Version.) If an optative represents a remote possibility, then a negative optative represents a wish that there not even be the remotest possibility that the event could actually occur. For this kind of construction, a negative subjunctive would not be strong enough, so even at a time when the optative was fading from view in the Greek language, it was still retained in an expression such as this. In the Vulgate, μὴ γένοιτο [mē genoito] is translated as *absit*, a present subjunctive form that is not really as strong but expresses the idea as well as Latin is able to.

Mood in Subordinate Clauses

The Greek and Latin names for the subjunctive (ὑποστατική [hypostatikē] and subiunctivus) both mean "subordinate," and in the vast majority of cases, the subjunctive and optative appear in subordinate clauses, rather than in independent ones. As these two moods occur in subordinate clauses, they can indicate either a conceptual subordination of one idea to another or a purely grammatical subordination of one clause to another. When the two moods indicate conceptual subordination, there are many nuances that they convey in particular constructions, and you will need to spend a fair bit of time later in your Greek or Latin career learning these various nuances. I will return to some of these nuances in part 4, but for now it is sufficient to note that if you remember the basic idea that the subjunctive is for less than certain events and the optative (if it exists) is for still more remote possibilities, this will give you a framework in which to place the various specific uses you will have to learn. Nevertheless, it is worth writing a few more words now about grammatical subordination.

In the previous chapter I introduced the idea of consecution or sequence of time by using the illustration "Glenn says that it is raining." The time referent of the verb "is" indicates that it is raining at the time Glenn is speaking. If one changes the time referent of the verb "says" (from present to past, for example), one also has to change the verb "is." During that discussion, I deliberately used the phrase "consecution (sequence) of time," even though the English grammatical term is "consecution/ sequence of tenses." Part of my reason for doing this was that I had not yet covered tenses per se, and I did not want to use a technical term that I was not yet ready to describe. My greater reason for doing this was that in Greek and Latin, consecution of verbs does not involve tense alone; it may also involve mood, since as you now know, tense and mood are very closely connected. To say this a different way, when one changes the tense of the main verb ("says" in the example above), in Greek or Latin one may need to change either the tense or the mood of the verb in the subordinate clause ("is raining"). Let me illustrate how this would work first in Latin and then in Greek, to give you an idea of what is involved.

In classical Latin, one could not actually say, "Glenn says that it is raining." One would have to say the equivalent of "Glenn says it to be raining." In later Latin, under the influence of the Greek New Testament, it is much more common to say, "Glenn says that it is raining." In this case, the verb "is raining" could be in either the indicative mood or the subjunctive mood. If it is subjunctive, the point is simply that this clause is grammatically subordinated to the main clause. If one then switches to the past ("Glenn said that it was raining"), one would change the verb of the main clause to the perfect indicative and the verb of the subordinate clause to the imperfect (either indicative or subjunctive). Similarly, if one wants to say, "Glenn said that it would be raining," in later Latin one would change the tense of the main verb to the perfect indicative and the verb of the subordinate clause would be in the imperfect subjunctive to indicate that the time of the rain was subsequent to the time Glenn was speaking and was possible, rather than actual. So Latin consecutes its tenses the same way English does (it makes adjustments to the tense of the verb in the subordinate clause when the tense of the main clause verb changes), although it often also uses the subjunctive mood to show grammatical subordination.

In contrast to the way later Latin works, if one wants to say, "Glenn says that it is raining" in Greek, one must put the verb "is raining" in the present indicative. One cannot use the subjunctive for grammatical subordination here. If one changes the sentence to the past ("Glenn said that it was raining"), then the verb "is raining" must stay in the present tense, because the action of rain is happening at the same time Glenn is speaking, even though his speaking is in the past, but one may put the verb "is raining" in the optative mood to indicate its grammatical subordination to the main clause, whose verb is in the past.[9] Conversely, if one takes the statement "Glenn says that it will be raining" and transposes that to the past ("Glenn said that it

9. In New Testament Greek, one could use either the subjunctive or the indicative here.

would be raining"), then the verb "is raining" must be in the future optative (future because the action of raining is subsequent to the action of speaking, but optative because of the grammatical subordination to the main clause whose verb is in the past). This probably sounds extremely complicated to you at this point, and if you are studying *koine* Greek, you may be glad you do not have to learn the optative! The point, though, is that in Greek, consecution/sequence has more to do with moods than with tenses. The tenses change less than they do in Latin or English, and grammatical subordination is indicated by changes in mood.

Again, there are many variations in the way the tenses and moods work together in different kinds of Greek and Latin sentences, and I will return to those variations later. My purpose in this section has been simply to alert you to the fact that the use of the subjunctive or optative may indicate nothing more than grammatical subordination of one clause to another, or it may have more of a conceptual significance, a significance that would then need to be reflected in the English translation of the sentence. Recognizing that either grammatical or conceptual subordination may be at work with verbs in these moods should help you to understand the specific uses that you will have to learn for each mood.

Formation of Greek and Latin Verbs

At this point, you may be in shock over how many different verb forms you are going to have to learn. In fact, you may have been in shock since the last chapter! So it is probably well past time to reassure you that learning the forms of Greek and Latin verbs is not as hard as it may seem at the moment. You do not have to memorize hundreds of unrelated forms for the persons, numbers, tenses, moods, and voices. Instead, just as Greek and Latin noun and adjective forms are produced by adding different gender, case, and number endings to the root, so also verbs in the classical languages are formed by making regular, logical changes to the root. Let us look briefly at how the forms are constructed in each language.

Latin Verb Formation

In the case of Latin verbs, these changes consist of three types: stem changes, additions to the stem, and endings. From the root of a Latin verb, one builds three different **stems**: the present stem, the perfect active stem, and the perfect passive stem. For example, the root of *amo* ("I love") is *am-*, and from this root are built the three stems. The present stem is the same: *am-*. The perfect active stem is *amav-*, and the perfect passive stem is *amat-*. Then to these stems one adds additional markers that indicate different tenses and moods. Finally, one adds endings that indicate the person, number, and voice. So if one wants to form the third person singular pluperfect indicative active of *amo* (which would translate as "he/she had loved"), then one takes *amav-* (perfect active stem) + *-era-* (the sign of the pluperfect indicative) + *-t* (the ending for third person singular active). Thus, the form is *amaverat*. Conversely, if one sees *amaverat*, then one looks at *am-* to find the root and recognize the word and its basic usage, then one looks at *-av-* to recognize the perfect active stem, then at *-era-* to recognize that it is pluperfect, and finally at *-t* to know that it is third person singular active.

To help you remember the different stems of each verb (and to alert you to the presence of irregularities in stem formation), your vocabulary entry for each Latin verb will eventually include four forms, called **principal parts**. Table 7-7 (page 134) indicates the principal parts of a Latin verb and their significance.

Furthermore, in Latin, just as there are different declensions of nouns and adjectives, so also there are four **conjugations of verbs**. These patterns differ primarily in the vowels they use just prior to the ending. (There are also some differences in which letters they add to the stem to indicate the various tenses and moods.) For example, *laudo* ("I praise") is a **first-conjugation** verb, which in the present indicative has an *-a-* before the ending (in most cases): the third person singular present indicative active is *laudat*. In contrast, a **second-conjugation** verb like *habeo* ("I have") has an *-e-* before the ending: *habet*. A third-conjugation verb like *dico* ("I say") has various vowels before the ending; in the third person singular the vowel is *-i-*: *dicit*. A **fourth-conjugation** verb like *audio* ("I hear") has an *-i-*: *audit*. One can

Table 7-7: Principal Parts of Latin Verbs

Principal Part	Form	Significance
First	1st person singular present indicative active ("I do")	Lexical form of the verb that will be listed in dictionaries
Second	present active infinitive ("to do")	Source of the present stem; indication of the conjugation (1st, 2nd, 3rd, or 4th)
Third	1st person singular perfect indicative active ("I did")	Source of the perfect active stem
Fourth	nominative masculine singular perfect passive participle ("done")	Source of the perfect passive stem

recognize the conjugation of a verb by the form of the present active infinitive, which is the second principal part.

Greek Verb Formation

With Greek verbs, the situation is very similar, except that additions are made to the beginning of the root as well as the end. These changes to the front of the root can take the form of either **augment** or **reduplication**. Augment is the addition of an ε (epsilon—equivalent to an "e") in front of the root of a verb, or, if the verb root begins with a vowel, the lengthening of that vowel. Reduplication is the addition of a syllable to the front of the root, and this syllable consists of the initial consonant of the root (sometimes slightly modified), plus an ε. (Or if the root begins with a vowel, that vowel is lengthened. In this case, reduplication looks the same as augment.) For example, in the case of the verb παιδεύω [*paideuo*], which means "I teach," the root is παι-δευ- [*paideu-*], the augmented form of the root is ἐπαιδευ- [*epaid-eu*], and the reduplicated form is πεπαιδευ- [*pepaideu-*]. Augment and reduplication are used to form various stems of Greek verbs. The verbs also add markers after the stem to indicate tense and

Table 7-8 Principal Parts of Greek Verbs

Principal Part	Form	Significance
First	1st person singular present indicative active ("I do")	Lexical form of the verb that will be listed in dictionaries; also indicates the type or conjugation of the verb and serves as the source of the present stem
Second	1st person singular future indicative active ("I will do")	Source of the future active/middle stem
Third	1st person singular aorist indicative active ("I did")	Source of the aorist active stem
Fourth	1st person singular perfect indicative active ("I have done")	Source of the perfect active stem
Fifth	1st person singular perfect indicative middle/passive ("I have done to myself"; "I have been done")	Source of the perfect middle/passive stem
Sixth	1st person singular aorist indicative passive ("I was done")	Source of the aorist passive stem

mood, just as Latin verbs do, and they add endings that indicate person, number, and voice.

In keeping with the fact that Greek verbs have more forms than Latin verbs, Greek verbs have six different stems and thus six principal parts that will be part of the vocabulary entry for each verb. The principal parts are listed in table 7-8.

In Greek there are three different patterns or conjugations of verbs. These are labeled not with numbers, but by their names, and the names reflect the ending used in the first person singular present indicative active (the first principal part). The most common pattern of verbs is called **omega verbs**, whose first principal part ends in the letter ω (omega—equivalent to a long "o"). A second pattern is called **contract verbs**, that is, verbs whose stems end in a vowel—ε (epsilon), ο (omicron), or α (alpha), and that vowel contracts with the vowel of the ending to make a different vowel. (Some textbooks of New Testament Greek refer to contract verbs by the vowel prior to the ending omega: -εω or "epsilon-omega verbs," -οω or "omicron-omega verbs," and -αω or "alpha-omega verbs.") The final (and least common) pattern is called **mi verbs**, because their ending in the first principal part is -μι (mu-iota) rather than ω.

In this chapter I have sought to build on the general understanding of verbs developed in the previous chapter by focusing on the most complicated elements of Greek and Latin finite verbs: tense and mood. I have also briefly explained how the verb forms are constructed from roots, stems (including augment and reduplication in the case of Greek verbs), and endings (both additions to indicate tense and mood, and endings to indicate person, number, and voice). It should be clear from this discussion that Greek or Latin verbs will require a great deal of effort for you to master, but this general overview should give you hooks on which to hang the specific pieces of information you will have to learn. Nevertheless, the finite verb forms are not the whole story of Greek and Latin verbs. In the next chapter I will direct our attention to the non-finite verb forms: infinitives and participles.

APPENDIX: GRAMMATICAL TERMS INTRODUCED IN CHAPTER 7

Aorist tense: In Greek, a grammatical category indicating that the event a verb describes took place in past time and that the event was considered as a whole, without regard to whether it was ongoing or completed (e.g., "he did").

Augment: In Greek, the addition of an ε (epsilon—equivalent to an "e") in front of the root of a verb, or if the verb root begins with a vowel, the lengthening of that vowel.

Contract verbs: In Greek, a group of verbs whose roots end in α (alpha), o (omicron), or ε (epsilon). In these verbs, the final vowel of the root contracts with the vowel of the ending to produce a different vowel.

First conjugation: In Latin, a group of verbs whose present active infinitive ends in -*āre* and that use the vowel "a" before the endings in the present indicative.

Fourth conjugation: In Latin, a group of verbs whose present active infinitive end in -*īre* and that use the vowel "i" before the endings in the present indicative.

Future perfect tense: In Greek and Latin, a grammatical category indicating that the event a verb describes will take place in future time and that that event will be completed prior to another event farther in the future (e.g., "he will have done"). This tense is extremely rare in later Greek.

Future tense: In Greek and Latin, a grammatical category indicating that the event a verb describes will take place in future time and that that event will be ongoing (e.g., "he will be doing"). Because the future perfect tense is so rare in later Greek, the future tense of that language often loses its aspect specificity and conveys simple aspect ("he will do") rather than specifically ongoing aspect.

Imperfect tense: In Greek and Latin, a grammatical category indicating that the event a verb describes took place in past time and that that event was ongoing (e.g., "he was doing").

Mi verbs: In Greek, a group of verbs whose forms end in the letters μι (mu-iota) in the first person singular present indicative active.

Omega verbs: In Greek, a group of verbs whose forms end in the letter ω (omega) in the first person singular present indicative active. This is the most common group of verbs in Greek.

Perfect tense: In Greek, a grammatical category indicating that the event a verb describes has been completed in past time and that its effects are ongoing in the present (e.g., "he has done"). In Latin, the perfect tense can indicate any event that took place in past time, whether one views it as a whole or considers its ongoing effects (e.g., "he has done," "he did").

Pluperfect tense: In Greek and Latin, a grammatical category indicating that the event a verb describes took place in past time and that that event was already completed at a later point in the past (e.g., "he had done"). This tense is rare in later Greek.

Present tense: In Greek and Latin, a grammatical category indicating that the event a verb describes takes place in present time and that that event is ongoing (e.g., "he is doing").

Principal parts: Basic forms of a Greek or Latin verb that enable one to know how its stems change, and thus how to produce other forms of the verb. Latin verbs normally have four principal parts; Greek verbs usually have six.

Reduplication: In Greek, the addition of a syllable to the front of a root or the lengthening of the initial vowel of the root. The added syllable consists of the root's initial consonant (sometimes modified, as, for example, when an initial φ [phi] becomes a π [pi] in reduplication), followed by the letter ε (epsilon).

Root: The base of a Greek or Latin verb, which determines the verb's usage (meaning). Verb forms are produced by modifying the root to make various stems and by adding various endings to the stems.

Second conjugation: In Latin, a group of verbs whose present active infinitive ends in -*ēre* and that use the vowel "e" before the endings in the present indicative.

Stem: A building block for verb forms. The stem is composed of the verb's root and various changes to that root (augment, reduplication, and/or additions at the end of the root), and endings are added to the stem to produce the varied forms.

Third conjugation: In Latin, a group of verbs whose present active infinitive ends in -*ere* and that use varied vowels before the endings in the present indicative.

8

SPECIAL (NON-FINITE) VERBAL FORMS

Infinitives and Participles

By now it should be clear that Greek and Latin verbs present challenges to English speakers in several ways. First, it is a challenge to recognize the verb forms, since they are marked by changes within the word, rather than by the addition of helping verbs as in English. Second, it is a challenge to understand the time and aspect indicated by different Greek and Latin tenses, since these do not line up very closely with English verb tenses. Third, it is a challenge to recognize the uses of the subjunctive mood (and, in the case of Greek, the optative), since we are losing our subjunctive in English today. It should also be clear, however, that these challenges have to do with the differences between Greek and Latin on one hand and English on the other. The challenges do not arise from any incoherence about the way Greek and Latin work. If one seeks to understand the classical languages on their own terms, it is by no means impossible to grasp the way they function. The classical languages are complex, but there is a logic to their complexity, and even an elegance about the way they work that in many ways English cannot match.

It is now time to turn our attention to the final challenge that awaits an English speaker learning the Greek or Latin verb system: the fact that these two languages use non-finite verbal forms much more extensively than English does. Here as well, though, there is some good news to go along with the challenge. Greek and Latin infinitives and participles actually work quite similarly to English infinitives and participles. The difference is that the classical languages have more of them (or at least more than we realize we have in English) and that they use them in situations where English would demand that we use subordinate clauses. So if you can recognize how English infinitives and participles work, even though we do not use them often, you will also be able to recognize how Latin and Greek non-finite verbal forms work. This is the task to which we turn in this chapter.

Infinitives: Verb Forms Used as Nouns

As you now know, a non-finite verbal form is a form that is not limited to a particular person. Naturally, another name for "non-finite" is "infinite," and thus it should be apparent that the **infinitive** is the non-finite verb form *par excellence,* because it is almost completely unlimited by its form. In English grammar, we generally say that we have only one infinitive, and this is the lexical form of a verb: "to swim," "to give," "to be." Thus, in English as we choose to describe it, the infinitive carries with it no time, person, or number reference. Actually, however, we have verb forms that correspond to infinitives and that refer to present, past, and future time, but we simply do not choose to call them infinitives. Consider the following phrases: "to be doing," "to have done," "to be about to do." These compound forms in English work like infinitives in Greek and Latin, and they correspond to present, past, and future time, just as Greek and Latin infinitives do. Furthermore, English has infinitive-like forms that are passive, rather than active: "to be done," "to have been done," "to be about to be done." We do not use these phrases very often, but we can understand them perfectly well.

Once one recognizes that we can use infinitive-type forms to indicate both active and passive action in the present, the past, or the future, then one is ready to understand Latin infinitives, which are presented in table 8-1.

Notice that, as shown in this table, Latin infinitives do not convey aspect. In other words, the infinitive does not indicate whether the action is ongoing or completed. If it is crucial to indicate aspect, and if the aspect is not obvious from the context,

Table 8-1 Latin Infinitives

Time Reference	Active Action	Passive Action
Present	*Present Active Infinitive* ("to be doing," "to do")	*Present Passive Infinitive* ("to be done")
Past	*Perfect Active Infinitive* ("to have done," "to have been doing")	*Perfect Passive Infinitive* ("to have been done")
Future	*Future Active Infinitive* ("to be about to do," "to be about to be doing")	*Future Passive Infinitive* ("to be about to be done")

then a Latin speaker/writer must recast the sentence using a finite verb form rather than an infinitive. One should remember that Latin verb tenses in general convey time more than aspect, and so it should not be surprising that Latin infinitives have no element of aspect at all. Accordingly, there are no imperfect, pluperfect, or future perfect infinitives in Latin.

In contrast, Greek verbs are more focused on aspect than Latin verbs are, so one should not be surprised that in Greek the infinitives focus primarily on aspect, rather than on time. Remember that the distinction between the aorist and the perfect tenses in Greek is one of aspect (the aorist conveys action with no reference to whether it is completed or ongoing, and the perfect refers to past action that is completed, but whose effects continue), and so the aorist and perfect infinitives can convey the same information about aspect that finite verbs in those tenses convey. Because of this emphasis on aspect, the Greek infinitive that most directly corresponds to the English "to do" is not the present, but the aorist, since the aorist indicates unspecified aspect. Furthermore, Greek verbs have a middle voice as well as an active and a passive voice, and thus there are infinitives in the middle voice, as well. Table 8-2 (page 142) indicates the possibilities for Greek infinitives, arranged by aspect and voice, rather than by time and voice. (I switch from "to do" to "to hit"

Table 8-2   Greek Infinitives

Aspect Reference	Active Action	Middle Action	Passive Action
Unspecified	*Aorist Active Infinitive* ("to hit")	*Aorist Middle Infinitive* ("to hit oneself")	*Aorist Passive Infinitive* ("to be hit")
On-Going	*Present Active Infin.* ("to be hitting")	*Present Middle Infin.* ("to be hitting oneself")	*Present Passive Infin.* ("to be getting hit")
	Future Active Infin ("to be about to hit")	*Future Middle Infin.* ("to be about to hit oneself")	*Future Passive Infin.* ("to be about to get hit")
Completed	*Perfect Active Infin.* ("to have hit")	*Perfect Middle Infin.* ("to have hit oneself")	*Perfect Passive Infin.* ("to have been hit")

in the English equivalents, in order to be able to indicate middle voice more easily).[1]

Because of the way infinitives function, grammarians refer to them as **verbal nouns**—that is, an infinitive is a verb used as a noun. In Greek and Latin, there are three major ways to use infinitives, two of which are possible in English, as well. First, one may use an infinitive as the subject of the sentence. When one says, "to swim is the best form of exercise," the phrase "to swim" is an infinitive, yet it is used as the subject of the verb "is." The infinitive answers the question "What?" What is the best form of exercise? To swim is the best form of exercise. You will notice here that saying "to swim" in this illustration is a little bit unnatural. We would be more likely to say "Swimming is the best form of exercise." I will return to the question of what kind of word "swimming" is later in this chapter, but the reason I have used an odd example is that in Greek and Latin, much more often than in English, infinitives are used as the subjects

---

1. In addition to the infinitives listed in table 8-2, there is also a future perfect infinitive, but this is quite rare even in early Greek, and virtually nonexistent in later Greek.

of sentences—that is, in Greek and Latin, one says, "To do this is better than to do that," or "To be a teacher is a noble profession," whereas in English, we are more likely to say "doing" or "being" in these instances.

Second, one may use the infinitive to complete the meaning of certain verbs. When one says, "I am starting to do my homework," the phrase "to do my homework" is an infinitive phrase that completes the meaning of "starting." Latin uses its present infinitive and Greek its present or aorist infinitive in the same way as the English infinitive is used in this example. In this case, the infinitive is still functioning as a noun, and it still answers the question "What?" What am I starting to do? I am starting to do my homework. Thus one could say grammatically that in this case, the infinitive phrase is the object of the verb "start."

A third way of using infinitives in Greek and Latin is in indirect statements. Consider the following sentence: "She says that we will go to the mall today." In Greek and Latin, one could say this sentence like this: "She says us to be about to go to the mall today." In fact, in early Latin, this would be the way one had to say it. In this kind of construction, the subject of the infinitive, "us," goes in the accusative case in Greek or Latin, and the tense of the infinitive is determined by the time or aspect it needs to convey. So the equivalent of "to be about to go" would be a future active infinitive in Latin or Greek. The fact that Greek and Latin use infinitives in indirect statements is the main reason they need to have so many tenses of infinitives. The tenses are necessary to convey the relation between the action of the main verb and the action of the infinitive, both in terms of time and in terms of aspect (especially in Greek). Notice that if one said, "She says us to go to the mall today" (with no clear time or aspect relationship between the saying and the going), the sentence would be very poor and ambiguous. Greek and Latin use infinitives of various tenses to express precisely the relation between the two actions of this sentence. English, in contrast, does the same thing by using a subordinate clause, "that we will go," so that there will be a finite verb more capable of expressing the time/aspect relation.

Notice here that Greek and Latin can use an infinitive phrase where English usually needs a subordinate clause. The difference lies not so much in how the infinitives work as in how frequently they are used. In the New Testament, a noteworthy example of this comes in Jesus' famous question to the disciples, "Who do you say that I am?" (Matthew 16:15). In English, the indirect question requires a subordinate clause: "that I am." In both the Greek New Testament and the Latin Vulgate, however, this question is handled with an infinitive phrase using an accusative personal pronoun (spelled *me* in Latin and με [*me*] in Greek) and a present infinitive (εἶναι [*einai*] in Greek, *esse* in Latin): "Who do you say me to be?" Notice also, however, that there are some cases where English uses an infinitive phrase, where Latin and Greek must use a subordinate clause. In the sentence "I want you to do this for me," the phrase "you to do this for me" is an infinitive phrase used to complete the meaning of the verb "want." As we have seen, though, Greek and Latin do not normally do this. Instead, they say, "I want that you do this for me." So part of learning to work with Greek and Latin infinitives is recognizing when those languages can use an infinitive phrase and when they must use a subordinate clause. Different situations call for different grammatical constructions, and in some cases, as we have just seen, Greek and Latin prefer one construction, where English prefers the other.

Participles: Verb Forms Used as Adjectives

If an infinitive is a verbal noun, a participle is a **verbal adjective**—that is, a verb form used as an adjective. Consider again an illustration from chapter 3: "Give the book to the not-so-tall girl talking too noisily over there." In that sentence, "talking too noisily over there" is a participial phrase modifying "girl." "Talking" is a verb form that can function as an adjective. Here one should remember that, unlike English, Greek and Latin decline their adjectives—that is, their adjectives have distinct forms for masculine, feminine, and neuter gender, for singular, [dual], and plural number, and for the various cases. Likewise, Greek and Latin participles also have endings for gender, number, and case. In other words, the endings of these words look very similar to the endings on adjectives in the classical languages. So if one wanted to write "Give the book to the not-so-tall girl talking too noisily over there" in Greek or Latin, the word "talking" would have to be feminine singular in form, since it modifies "girl," and it would have to be in the dative case, since the idea of "to the girl" would be expressed by a noun in the dative case in Greek or Latin. Because the form of "talking" would clearly link it to "girl," one could put the word "talking" somewhere else besides next to "girl," and the meaning would still be clear. In fact, the most common order in which to write this in Greek would be "to the too-noisily over there talking girl." In Latin, the most common order would be "to [the] girl too noisily over there talking."

English has only two participles: the present participle ("doing") and the past participle ("done"). As was the case with infinitives, so also here, English can use helping words to make phrases that function like participles in various tenses and in both active and passive voice. For example, the phrases "about to be doing" and "about to be done" convey future ideas, "having done" and "having been done" convey past ideas, and "doing" and "being done" convey present ideas.

We can expect Latin participles to convey time and Greek participles to convey aspect, just as the infinitives in the respective languages do. Accordingly, there are Greek participles indicating unspecified aspect, ongoing aspect, and completed aspect, as well as active, middle, and passive action, and Greek possesses participles in the same four tenses for which it possesses infinitives (present, aorist, perfect, and future).[2] Table 8-3 (page 146) shows the Greek participles and indicates which set of adjective endings each participle uses.

One should notice that there is a great deal of imprecision when one renders the Greek participles in English. The difference between the present, aorist, and perfect participles has more to do with aspect than with time, so one could render the aorist

2. Just as there is a future perfect infinitive in early Greek, so also is there a future perfect participle, but again, it is rare even in the early period, and virtually disappears later.

Table 8-3 Greek Participles

Aspect Reference	Active Action	Middle Action	Passive Action
Unspecified	Aorist Active Part. 1st/3rd declen. endings ("hitting")	Aorist Middle Part. 1st/2nd declen. endings ("hitting oneself")	Aorist Passive Part. 1st/3rd declen. endings ("being hit")
On-Going	Present Active Part. 1st/3rd declen. endings ("hitting")	Present Middle Part. 1st/2nd declen. endings ("hitting oneself")	Present Passive Part. 1st/2nd declen. endings ("being hit")
	Future Active Part 1st/3rd declen. endings ("being about to hit")	Future Middle Part. 1st/2nd declen. endings ("being about to hit oneself")	Future Passive Part. 1st/2nd declen. endings ("being about to get hit")
Completed	Perfect Active Part. 1st/3rd declen. endings ("having hit")	Perfect Middle Part. 1st/2nd declen. endings ("having hit oneself")	Perfect Passive Part. 1st/2nd declen. endings ("having been hit")

active participle either as "hitting" or as "having hit," depending on the context. In either case, though, the aorist participle is looking at an action as a whole, rather than indicating whether it is completed or ongoing. The present and future participles envision ongoing action, and the perfect participle indicates completed action with ongoing results. In terms of the relation between time and aspect, Greek participles mirror Greek infinitives.

In light of the way Greek participles function, one might expect Latin participles to function in the same way as the six Latin infinitives. In fact, however, Latin uses only four participles; it is missing the expected present passive and perfect active participles. It possesses present active participles (equivalent to "doing") and perfect passive participles (equivalent to "having been done"), and these work as one would expect, with more of a time reference than an aspect reference. The two future participles in Latin have special nuances, though. The future active participle indicates that an action is imminent ("about to do *soon*"), and the future passive participle indicates need or necessity (*"needing* to be done"). One can remember these two participial constructions through two well-known phrases. One line of the Nicene Creed declares that Jesus "is coming again." In the Latin version of the Creed, this line reads *et iterum venturus est,* in which *venturus* is a future active participle indicating that Jesus is "about to come." An even more familiar aid exists for remembering the future passive participle. The English word "agenda" is actually the Latin neuter plural future passive participle of the verb for "to do." *Agenda* in Latin means "the things needing to be done."

A well-known line from the fifth-century Latin hymn *Te Deum* illustrates the nuances of both of these Latin participles. The line, spoken as a prayer to God the Son, reads as follows: *Tu ad liberandum suscepturus hominem non horruisti virginis uterum.* The main clause of this sentence is *tu . . . non horruisti virginis uterum,* which means, "you . . . did not despise the virgin's womb." Between the subject (*tu*) and the main verb (*horruisti*) are two verbal phrases that both modify *tu* adjectivally. The first is *ad liberandum hominem,* and the second is *suscepturus hominem.* (Notice that the word *hominem*—"man"—is the object of both verbal forms, even though it is written only once.) In the first phrase, *liberandum* is a future passive participle, so the idea of this phrase is "for the purpose of man needing to be freed."[3] Notice here that the future passive participle indicates obligation as well as future time and passive action. Mankind needs to be set free from sin. In the second phrase, *suscepturus* is a future active participle, and the idea is "as you [were] about to assume man." In this case, notice that imminence is implied: just as God the Son was about to assume humanity through the incarnation, he did not despise or reject the prospect of entering the virgin's womb. So this sentence comes together rather literally as "You, when you were about to assume humanity, for the

3. The future passive participle is sometimes called a **gerundive.** One can construe a gerundive as the normal use of the future passive participle (a passive adjective expressing need or obligation), as I have done in the text. However, some grammarians construe a gerundive in a way more akin to a gerund, which I will discuss later in this chapter.

Table 8-4 Latin Participles

Time Reference	Active Action	Passive Action
Present	*Present Active Participle* 3rd declension endings ("doing")	——
Past	——	*Perfect Passive Participle* 1st/2nd declension endings ("having been done")
Future	*Future Active Participle* 1st/2nd declension endings ("about to do [soon]")	*Future Passive Participle* 1st/2nd declension endings ("needing to be done")

sake of humanity needing to be set free, you did not despise the virgin's womb." Then in better English, this becomes, "As you were about to assume humanity in order to set humanity free, you did not despise the virgin's womb."

Table 8-4 indicates the Latin participles and the endings they use. Notice once again the special nuances of the future participles.

Using Participles as Nouns

We have seen that infinitives are verbal nouns and participles are verbal adjectives. We should also recognize, however, that in Greek and Latin, adjectives can function as nouns. So if a participle is a verb that is used as an adjective, and if an adjective can be used as a noun, then a participle can also be used as a noun. (In this case, it is called a **substantive participle**.) Consider again the awkward illustration above: "To swim is the best form of exercise." As I wrote earlier, the way we would normally say this is, "Swimming is the best form of exercise." In this case, "swimming" is a present participle used as the subject of a sentence.[4]

4. In English grammar, a present participle used as a noun is called a "gerund." As we shall see, however, the grammatical term "gerund" refers to a more specific kind of construction in Latin than it does in English, and in

As we saw above, in Greek and Latin one would use an infinitive here ("to swim is . . ."), but if one wanted to say "The man who is swimming in that lake is in very good shape," one would use a present participle for "the man who is swimming." Greek does this much more often than Latin, since Greek can use the definite article to mark a participle as a substantive. Latin, since it has no article, is more likely to use a relative clause. So in this case, in Greek one would say, "The swimming-in-that-lake-man is in very good shape," but in Latin (like English) one would say, "That man who is swimming in that lake is in very good shape." In Latin, for one to be able to use a participle substantively, it must be clear from the context that the participle is meant as a noun. Overall, Latin resorts to relative clauses in many cases, when Greek can conveniently use a participle with an article in front of it.

As an illustration of the differences between Greek and Latin here, consider these two New Testament passages. In Philippians 1:1, Paul writes, "To all the saints in Christ Jesus who are at Philippi." Just after the Annunciation, Mary praises God by saying in Luke 1:50: "His mercy is on those who fear him from generation to generation." In the first passage in Greek, the phrase translated "who are at Philippi" is a participial phrase consisting of the definite article and a present participle ("the [ones] being at Philippi"). The lack of an article in Latin forces the translator to render the passage with a relative clause: "who are at Philippi." Here Greek and Latin must work differently because it is harder for Latin to indicate a substantive use of a participle. In the second passage, however, the phrase rendered "on those who fear him" includes a substantive participle ("the [ones] fearing him" in Greek and "[ones] fearing him" in Latin) in both languages. In this case, the use of the dative case (*to* ones fearing) makes it clear enough that the participle is substantive, and so Latin is able to use the participle, even though it has no article to mark it off. Thus, in some cases, Greek and Latin are both able to use a substantive participle, but in most cases Greek may do

keeping with my normal pattern, in the text I will introduce the term "gerund" only in connection with its Latin usage, not in connection with its English usage.

so, but Latin needs to recast the participial phrase into a relative clause.[5]

If a participle may be used as a noun, then there is obviously overlap between verbal nouns and verbal adjectives. One consequence of this overlap is that Latin can use a verbal form that looks like a neuter singular future passive participle to take the place of the present active infinitive. This verbal noun is called a **gerund**. It is always active in meaning and is always used in cases other than the nominative. Remember that an infinitive has no case endings, and so in Latin an infinitive functions as a noun in the nominative case. (As we shall see in chapter 9, Greek can use an infinitive in any case by putting an article in front of it.) If, in Latin, one needs to use a verbal form as a noun in some other case besides the nominative, then one uses a gerund. A well-known example of this is the early Church's slogan *lex orandi lex credendi*. Here, both *orandi* and *credendi* are gerunds (they look like neuter genitive singular future passive participles), and both are used as nouns. So this translates as "the law of praying [is] the law of believing," or, more expansively, "the way one prays shows what one believes." As you encounter gerunds in Latin, you will need to be on guard against the tendency to treat them as passive forms because they look like the future passive participle.

Identifying Verb Forms

In the three chapters dealing with verbs, we have seen how complex Greek and Latin verbs are. I hope that in the midst of that complexity, the inner logic of those verb systems has also become clearer. In any Indo-European language, verbs must explain what kind of action the sentence describes, who is doing the action, the attitude of the subject toward the action, the time of the action, and the aspect of the action. These questions lead to the basic grammatical information that verb forms convey: Finite verb forms indicate person, number, tense, mood, and voice. Non-finite verb forms do not technically have mood, but

---

5. This is part of why Latin, especially late Latin, is easier for English speakers. Latin uses almost as many relative clauses as English does, whereas Greek uses far fewer of them, and thus Greek is more foreign to us.

Figure 8-1 Identifying Greek or Latin Verb Forms

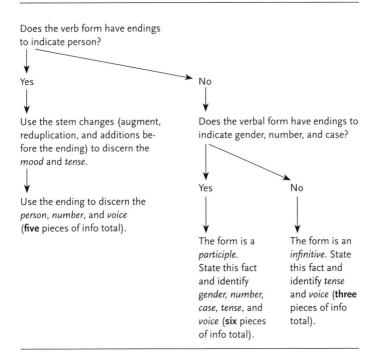

Does the verb form have endings to indicate person?

Yes → No

Yes: Use the stem changes (augment, reduplication, and additions before the ending) to discern the *mood* and *tense.*

Use the ending to discern the *person, number,* and *voice* (**five** pieces of info total).

No: Does the verbal form have endings to indicate gender, number, and case?

Yes — No

Yes: The form is a *participle.* State this fact and identify *gender, number, case, tense,* and *voice* (**six** pieces of info total).

No: The form is an *infinitive.* State this fact and identify *tense* and *voice* (**three** pieces of info total).

the categories (infinitive and participle) take the place of moods and often answer the syntax question, "What is the mood of this form?" Of the two non-finite verbal forms, infinitives have only tense and voice. Participles likewise have tense and voice, but because they function as adjectives, participles also have gender, number, and case.[6] Accordingly, as one examines a verb form in Greek or Latin, it is appropriate to begin by determining whether it is finite or non-finite. Finite verbs possess endings to indicate person; non-finite verbal forms do not. Once one has made this determination, one can identify the person, number, tense, mood, and voice of a finite verb form, the tense and voice of an infinitive, or the gender, number, case, tense, and voice of a participle. Figure 8-1 indicates a procedure one might follow.

6. By this logic, one might expect infinitives to have gender, number, and case, since they function as nouns. In fact, they do not.

At this point in our introduction to the way the classical languages work, we have looked primarily at the ways the various cases of nouns and adjectives function (in part 2) and the ways the various moods and non-finite verbal forms function (in part 3). As you solidify these concepts in your mind and learn the many forms that these inflected words (verbs, nouns, adjectives, articles, and pronouns) take, you will be well prepared to read increasingly complex sentences in Greek or Latin. Parts 2 and 3 have also included a fair bit of information about various ways to put sentences together (e.g., using a participial phrase in Greek or a relative clause in Latin to accomplish the same function). It is now time to turn from the words themselves to sentences as a whole. In part 4, I will discuss some of the main ideas sentences need to express and various ways of expressing these ideas. This will involve a bit of overlap with constructions we have already examined, and that overlap should help to solidify these ideas in your mind. I will also suggest some strategies for analyzing and understanding complex sentences.

APPENDIX: GRAMMATICAL TERMS INTRODUCED IN CHAPTER 8

Gerund: In Latin, a verbal noun (identical to a neuter singular future passive participle, but translated with an active meaning) that is used to replace a present active infinitive in a case besides the nominative.

Gerundive: In Latin, a future passive participle used to indicate that the action needs to be accomplished. This is the normal use of a future passive participle.

Infinitive: A non-finite verbal form that is used as a noun.

Substantive participle: A participle that is used to take the place of a noun.

Verbal adjective: A verbal form used as an adjective.

Verbal noun: A verbal form used as a noun.

PART 4 **LOOKING AT SENTENCES AS A WHOLE**

9

WORDS, PHRASES, CLAUSES

Putting Them Together

Even if one is working in a highly inflected language such as
Greek or Latin, sentences that express only a single thought are
relatively simple. Once one learns the vocabulary words, the case
endings, and the indicative verb forms, such sentences are not
at all difficult to translate. The complexity comes when Greek
or Latin authors combine multiple phrases and clauses, creating
long sentences (often much longer than we would be allowed to
use in English today) in which students often get quite lost. In
this part of the book, I hope to give you some guidance as you
develop your skill in navigating a Greek or Latin sentence. I will
try to do this in two ways: first (in this chapter) by continuing
my discussion of function—if one wants to say *this*, what are the
ways one can do so?—and then (in the last chapter) by suggest-
ing a strategy that you can use for analyzing the words in front
of you and determining how the author intended them to relate
to one another.

How, then, does one go about expressing complicated ideas?
In English, the primary way to do so is through clauses. Because
English has only a few remnants of a case system, and because
it does not often use participles to express ideas, it resorts to
clauses containing finite verb forms to express many of its major
ideas. You are familiar with independent clauses and subordinate clauses. You are also familiar with one type of subordinate
clause, called a relative clause. In addition to these, there are
various other kinds of subordinate clauses to indicate different

kinds of relations.[1] As you know by now, however, Latin and especially Greek are able to express many ideas using phrases that English must express with clauses. Therefore, in this chapter I will not divide my material in terms of kinds of clauses, but in terms of kinds of ideas that need to be expressed. You will need to recognize the Greek and Latin modes for expressing many different kinds of ideas, but I would like to concentrate on five of the most basic and most common. These are **purpose**, **result**, **time**, **cause** (and its reverse, **concession**), and **condition**. As I discuss each of these ideas, I will briefly mention the major way (not necessarily the only way) this idea is expressed in English and will then focus on the various ways one can express this idea in Greek and/or Latin. As I have mentioned above, this will involve overlap with some material I have covered earlier in this book, but this repetition should be beneficial, and this chapter should enable you to recognize more fully the fact that languages can perform the same function in a variety of ways. There is not an absolute standard for how one must express a given idea.

Expressing Purpose

One thing a sentence must do often is to convey the purpose for which the action of the main clause is being done. In English, we normally express such purpose using an infinitive phrase: "I am studying to do well on the exam." Of course, we could also say, "I am studying so that I may do well on the exam," although this is less common in English than an infinitive. In the classical languages, both of these are possible, but the second is greatly preferred. The following are the most common ways to express the purpose of an action in Greek or Latin. In each case, I will deal with how Greek or Latin would express the English ideas "Jesus *sends* the apostles to preach the gospel" and "Jesus *sent* the apostles to preach the gospel."

---

1. Some of these are temporal clauses, purpose clauses, result clauses, concessive clauses, and causal clauses. As usual, I will not define these terms until we encounter them in Greek or Latin grammar, later in this chapter.

Purpose Clause (in Greek or Latin). A **purpose clause** is a subordinate clause introduced by a subordinate conjunction equivalent to "so that" or "in order that" in English. In Latin the conjunction is usually *ut* (although it can also be *ne*); in Greek it may be ἵνα (*hina*), ὡς (*hōs*), or ὅπως (*hopōs*). The verb in the subordinate clause must be consecuted according to the rules of the language in question. Thus, in Greek there is a consecution/ sequence of *moods*, but in Latin there is a consecution of *tenses*. If one wants to say with reference to the present or the future, "Jesus *sends* the apostles so that they may preach the gospel," or "Jesus *will send* the apostles so that they may preach the gospel," then in Latin or Greek the verb for "may preach" would go in the present subjunctive. If, however, one wants to say with reference to a main verb in the past, "Jesus *sent* the apostles so that they might preach the gospel," then in this case, in Latin the verb for "might preach" would go in the imperfect subjunctive, but in Greek it would go in the future optative (future because the preaching comes after the sending; optative because the sending was in the past).[2]

Relative Clause (in Greek or Latin). One may use a relative clause when the people who will accomplish the purpose have already been specified. Thus in Greek or Latin one could say, "Jesus *sends* the apostles *who may preach* the gospel." In Latin, the verb for "may preach" would be in the present subjunctive, but in Greek the verb for "may preach" would be in the future indicative (future because the preaching is future to the sending). If one wanted to say with reference to the past, "Jesus *sent* the apostles *who might preach* the gospel," then in this case in Latin the verb for "might preach" would be in the imperfect subjunctive (imperfect because the main verb is in the past), but in Greek it would still be in the future indicative (because Greek does not consecute tenses as Latin and English do).

Infinitive Phrase (in Greek or Latin). This is quite rare, but it is possible in later Greek or later Latin to use an infinitive as Eng-

2. In New Testament Greek, this would normally be the present subjunctive rather than the future optative.

lish does: "Jesus sent the disciples *to preach* the gospel." In Latin, the infinitive would normally be in the present (although the very rare future infinitive would be possible), but in Greek the infinitive would more likely be aorist in order to emphasize the action of preaching most strongly.

Gerundive (in Latin only). As we have already seen, Latin can use a future passive participle with a noun to indicate purpose. One would thus say the equivalent of "Jesus sends the apostles *for the gospel needing to be preached*." In this case, the preposition "for" would be *ad*, which takes the accusative case. So both "gospel" and the future passive participle "needing to be preached" would be neuter accusative singular (neuter, because the word for "gospel" is neuter in Latin).

Articular Infinitive (in Greek only). An **articular infinitive** is the use of a neuter article with an infinitive. Because the article declines, the infinitive can then assume the case of the article (and thus the use of that case), even though it does not itself have case endings. An articular infinitive can be used in a variety of ways, but to express purpose, one would ordinarily use the preposition εἰς (*eis*), meaning "unto" or "for the purpose of," and this preposition takes the accusative case. So one would say the equivalent of "Jesus sends the apostles *unto the them to-preach of the gospel*." This is incomprehensible in English, but if one remembers that we use a gerund rather than an infinitive to make a verb into a noun, then one can understand this Greek sentence as the equivalent of "Jesus sends the apostles *unto the them preaching of the gospel*" or "Jesus sends the apostles *unto their preaching of the gospel*." One should notice that the Greek articular infinitive is somewhat comparable to the Latin gerundive, except that Greek uses an active form to express this idea, whereas Latin turns it around to use a passive form. In general, Latin uses passive forms far more often than Greek and English do.

Expressing Result

In many cases, expressions of result look a lot like expressions of purpose; the difference is that the result of an action is something that necessarily happened, whereas the purpose may or may not have actually happened. One can divide result into two subcategories, sometimes called **actual result** and **natural result**.

Actual result. This is the simple statement that "x" happened, and so "y" happened, as well. For instance, "Jesus was crucified, and so the disciples fled." This is expressed using a subordinate clause (usually introduced by ὥστε [hōste] in Greek or ut in Latin) and a verb in the indicative mood in Greek or the subjunctive mood in Latin. Thus, in Latin this construction looks very much like a purpose clause, except that the verb in the subordinate clause could be perfect subjunctive (as it would be in this case, "they fled"), rather than merely the present or the imperfect. In Latin the use of the subjunctive here simply indicates grammatical subordination of one clause to another, not conceptual subordination. In Greek the indicative mood indicates that the fleeing really happened.

Natural result. This sort of expression follows the form "so . . . that." For example, "Jesus was so clever that no one dared to answer his questions." Greek can express this using οὕτως (houtōs) . . . ὥστε (hōste) and either an infinitive or the indicative. Latin uses various words for "so" (tantus, tam, adeo, ita) and ut for "that," and once again it uses the subjunctive to indicate grammatical subordination of one clause to another.

Expressing Time

Whenever there are two or more actions in a sentence, it is important to indicate the relation between the time of the main clause's action and the time of the subordinate action. In English, this is almost always done by means of **temporal clauses**, which are subordinate clauses introduced by conjunctions with a time reference: "before," "after," "when," "while," "until." In Greek and Latin, there are two major ways to express the time relation between actions within a sentence.

Temporal Clause (in Greek or Latin). This clause works the same way in these two languages as it does in English. The subordinate conjunction indicates the relation between the time of the main clause and that of the temporal clause. In most cases, the verb in the temporal clause goes in the indicative mood, but there are a few other possibilities. In Latin the verb of the temporal clause can go in the subjunctive to indicate grammatical subordination of that clause to the main clause.[3] Also, in Greek when the conjunction is πρίν (*prin*), meaning "before," one can use the infinitive rather than an indicative verb form. A famous example of both of these patterns is Jesus' statement in John 8:58: "Before Abraham was, I am." In Greek, the conjunction πρίν (*prin*) is used with an aorist infinitive γενέσθαι (*genesthai*), meaning "was (born)," but in Latin this clause is written with an imperfect subjunctive verb, *fieret*.

Absolute Construction. Another common way to express the time relation between actions in a sentence is through an **ablative absolute** in Latin or a **genitive absolute** in Greek. Grammatically, the word "absolute" in the names of these constructions refers to a phrase that is not tied to the rest of the sentence grammatically. It is a phrase that stands on its own, even though it is not an independent clause. Absolute constructions are very rare in English today, although a hundred or more years ago, they were quite common. Consider the following two sentences: "The day being rainy, Camden did not go for a run," and "Being on the team, Justin had to practice even though it was raining." Neither of these is the way we would express these ideas today (we would virtually always use a clause introduced by the conjunction "since"), but both are comprehensible. In the second of these sentences, the participle "being" modifies the subject of the sentence, "Justin." So if English had distinct case endings, this participle would have to be nominative, since the subject is nominative. This is not an absolute construction, because the participle has a clear grammatical connection to the rest of the sentence—it modifies the sentence's subject. On the other hand, in the first sentence the participle "being" modifies "day," and

3. As we shall see below, with a subjunctive verb this construction could also indicate cause, rather than simple time.

"day" has no grammatical connection to the rest of the sentence. It has a conceptual connection (it explains why Camden did not go for a run), but not a grammatical connection. So this is an absolute construction.[4] In Greek and Latin, absolute constructions consist of a noun or pronoun and a participle (perhaps with other modifiers, as well), and they use the case for separation, since they are separate grammatically from the rest of the sentence. As you will remember, the separation case is the ablative in Latin and the genitive in Greek; hence the names "ablative absolute" and "genitive absolute" in the two languages.

In Greek, a genitive absolute can include a participle of any tense or any voice. That is, it can be active or passive (or, rarely, middle), and it can be present, aorist, future, or perfect. The tense of the participle can indicate the aspect relation (and to some degree, the time relation) between the genitive absolute and the rest of the sentence. So if one wanted to say, "The day being rainy, Camden did not go for a run" in Greek, one could use a present participle for "being" in order to show that the event of the absolute construction was ongoing and at the same time as the action of the main clause. Or, if one wanted to say, "The rain having ended, Camden went for a run," one could use an aorist participle for "having ended" to show that this action preceded the action of the main clause.

In Latin, the possibilities for an ablative absolute are more limited than in Greek. Remember that Latin has only four participles, and in fact only two of these are used in ablative absolutes: the present active participle and the perfect passive participle. So in Latin, one could not say, "The rain having ended, Camden went for a run." Instead, one would have to use a clause: "After the rain ended, Camden went for a run." One could say, "The day being rainy, Camden did not go for a run," using a present active participle for "being." One could also say, "The water having been removed from the court, Justin was able to play his tennis match," by using a perfect passive participle for "having been

4. In English grammar, this is called a "nominative absolute," because such constructions go in the nominative case if they involve pronouns, the only words left in English that still have distinct case endings.

removed." In Latin, most ablative absolutes use perfect passive participles,[5] another instance of the fact that Latin prefers the passive voice to the active. In the last example, English would invariably say, "After the officials removed the water from the court, Justin was able to play his tennis match" (a temporal clause with an active verb), Greek would probably say, "The officials having removed the water . . . , Justin was able to play. . . ." (a genitive absolute with an aorist active participle), and Latin would say, "The water having been removed . . . , Justin was able to play. . . ." (an ablative absolute with a perfect passive participle).

Expressing Cause or Concession

In the examples just above, the best way to render these Greek or Latin absolute constructions in English is not with the word "while" or "when," but with the word "since." This is because these constructions convey more than just a time relation between the two actions of the sentence; they also convey a causal relation. The reason Justin was able to play his tennis match, the cause of his being able to play the match, was that the officials had removed the water from the court. Grammatically, an ablative or genitive absolute does not clearly indicate cause, but in many instances the idea of the action in the absolute construction clearly relates to the idea of the main action in a causal way. Conversely, the relation between the absolute construction and the main action can be one of tension, rather than positive cause. For example, consider this sentence: "The court being dry, Justin still did not play the match." Here again we have an absolute construction, but the relation between it and the action of the main clause is one of logical tension. The court was dry, so Justin could have played the match, but he did not do so. This is referred to as a **concessive** idea, and in English, we would express it with a subordinate clause introduced by a word like "although"—"Although the court was dry, Justin still did not play the match."

In both Greek and Latin, absolute constructions can be used

5. The most famous counterexample is the well-known phrase *Deo volente,* which literally means "God being willing." This is an ablative absolute with a present active participle.

to express cause or concession, with the context and other marker words (corresponding to "still" in the previous example) serving to make clear whether the relation between the absolute construction and the main clause is one of time only, one of cause (equivalent to "since" or "because"), or one of concession (equivalent to "although" or "even though"). Because Greek has so many participles at its disposal, the genitive absolute is the *primary* way to express cause or concession in that language. Latin, with fewer participles, is much more likely to use a subordinate clause introduced by a conjunction meaning "since," "because," or "although." When Greek does use a subordinate clause, the verb is normally in the indicative. When Latin does so, the verb is usually in the subjunctive (although it can be in the indicative with certain conjunctions).

One other point is worth noting with respect to Latin. The most common subordinate conjunction in that language is *cum*, which can be used to mean "when," "since," or "although." (That is, it can express a time relation, a causal relation, or a concessive relation.) When *cum* is used with the indicative, it means "when" (a time relation). When it is used with the subjunctive, it can still mean simply "when" (in which case the subjunctive indicates grammatical subordination), or it can mean "since" (a causal relation). Only by context can one determine whether *cum* means "when" or "since" when used with a subjunctive verb. When *cum* is used with a subjunctive verb and the word *tamen* ("nevertheless") occurs in the main clause, then the idea is concessive: "Although the officials removed the water . . . , Justin *nevertheless* did not play his tennis match." Whereas English uses many different conjunctions to convey different relations between the subordinate clause and the main clause, Latin is able to use the same conjunction with different verb forms to indicate different relations. (Of course, Latin also has other subordinate conjunctions, as well.) In contrast, Greek usually conveys temporal, causal, and concessive relations using its genitive absolute construction.

Table 9-1 (page 164) indicates various ways to convey the relations of purpose, time, cause, and concession in Greek and Latin. This may serve as a convenient reference tool as you analyze Greek or Latin sentences.

Table 9-1 Expressing Purpose, Time, Cause, and Concession in Greek and Latin

Kind of Relation between Actions	Ways of Expressing this Relation in Greek	Ways of Expressing this Relation in Latin
Purpose	Purpose clause w/ pres. subjunctive or future optative	Purpose clause w/ present or imperfect subjunctive
	Relative clause w/ fut. indicative	Relative clause w/ present or imperfect subjunctive
	Articular infinitive	Gerundive
	Infinitive phrase (rare)	Infinitive phrase (rare)
Time	Temporal clause w/ indicative	Temporal clause w/ indic. or subj.
	Genitive absolute	Ablative absolute
	πρίν (*prin*) w/ infinitive	*Cum* w/ indicative or subjunctive
Cause	Genitive absolute	Ablative absolute
	Causal clause w/ indicative	Causal clause w/ subjunctive
		Cum w/ subjunctive
Concession	Genitive absolute	Ablative absolute
	Concessive clause w/ indicative	Concessive clause w/ subjunctive (usually) + *tamen* in main clause
		Cum w/ subjunctive + *tamen* in main clause

Expressing Condition

As I discussed verb moods in chapter 7, I began with the example of a sportscaster using the present tense to indicate a past contrary-to-fact event: "If he makes that block, they win the game," which, of course, should have been expressed, "If he had made that block, they would have won the game." This is an example of a **conditional sentence**, in which one clause expresses a condition, and the other clause expresses a result that will come about if the condition is met (or would have come about if the condition had been met). In grammatical terminology, the clause expressing the condition (that is, the "if" clause, although it can use another word like "unless" instead of "if") is called the **protasis**, and the clause expressing the result is called the **apodosis** You may need to learn these terms, but in this discussion I will simply refer to the "if clause" rather than "protasis" and the "main clause" rather than "apodosis."

Conditional sentences are normally classified according to how likely the condition is to be true or to be fulfilled (from the point of view of the speaker/writer). A condition can be **simple** (in which case the speaker passes no judgment about how likely the condition is to be fulfilled), **contrafactual** (in which case the speaker knows or assumes that the condition has not been met), **more vivid** (that is, quite likely to be fulfilled), or **less vivid** (that is, somewhat less likely to be fulfilled). Furthermore, a condition can refer to the past, the present, or the future. If it refers to the past or the present, then the categories of more vivid and less vivid do not apply; the condition was/is either fulfilled or it was/is not, even if the speaker does not know whether it was/is fulfilled. So past and present conditions include the categories of simple and contrafactual. If a condition applies to the future, then it cannot be contrafactual, since it has not yet been determined whether it will be fulfilled. So the condition can be either more vivid or less vivid, although Greek, with its greater verb precision, also includes a category of **most vivid**.

Remember that, in Latin, the indicative is for actions that are certain, and the subjunctive is for any action less than certain. So in Latin, simple conditions use the indicative mood. Furthermore, in order to distinguish between future conditions that are more vivid and those that are less vivid, Latin uses the indicative mood for the former and the subjunctive for the latter. Contrafactual conditions in Latin use the subjunctive. Thus, in a condition, a subjunctive referring to the future expresses a doubtful or possible outcome; a subjunctive referring to the present or past expresses a contrary-to-fact condition. Table 9-2 (page 166) lists the kinds of conditional sentences in Latin. Study this table carefully, noting the logic of the change from indicative to subjunctive and from one tense to another in different situations.

Table 9-2   Conditional Sentences in Latin

Type of Condition	Verb Form in If-Clause (Protasis)	Verb Form in Main Clause (Apodosis)
Present Simple ("If Paul is here, we are happy.")	Present Indicative	Present Indicative
Present Contrafactual ("If Paul were here, we would be happy.")	Imperfect Subjunctive	Imperfect Subjunctive
Past Simple ("If Paul was here, we were happy.")	Imperfect or Perfect Indicative	Imperfect or Perfect Indicative
Past Contrafactual ("If Paul had been here, we would have been happy.")	Pluperfect Subjunctive	Pluperfect Subjunctive
Future More Vivid ("If Paul comes, we will be happy.")	Future Indicative	Future Indicative (or Present Subjunctive)
Future Less Vivid ("If Paul should come, we would be happy.")	Present Subjunctive	Present Subjunctive (or Present Indicative)

The way Latin handles conditional sentences is fairly similar to the way English handles them.[6]

In Greek, the situation is different from Latin and English in four ways. First, as we have already seen, Greek consecutes moods more than tenses. Latin moves from one tense of the subjunctive to another in different situations, but in the same situations Greek moves from the subjunctive to the optative. Second, in Greek, a contrafactual condition is expressed with the indicative mood, not the optative or subjunctive. The reason for this is that if one knows a certain condition was not fulfilled or is not fulfilled, then one also knows what did happen or is hap-

6. The most noteworthy difference is that in English, the if clause of a future condition goes in the present tense, rather than the future. Notice the phrase "If Paul comes," where logically it should be "If Paul will come."

pening. So to the Greek mind, a contrafactual is just as "actual" as a factual condition; it is just that something else happened. So the optative is used for unlikely possibilities, the subjunctive for likely possibilities, and the indicative for contrafactual and factual events and for extremely likely possibilities in the future. Third, whereas Latin uses the same subordinate conjunction (*si*, meaning "if") in all cases, Greek uses different conjunctions and particles to express its subtle distinctions. Fourth, Greek distinguishes between a simple condition (which refers to a particular event/possibility, an event that happens once) and a general condition (which refers to a more generic, repeatable possibility in the present or the past). A general condition conveys the idea that "if x ever happens (or 'whenever x happens'), then y happens."

Table 9-3 (page 168) lists the kinds of conditional sentences in Greek (listed as they are normally described in classical Greek grammars) and gives both verb and particle information. Study it carefully, again noticing the logic of changing from one mood to another and one tense to another.

Students of *koine* Greek should also notice that in many New Testament Greek textbooks, simple conditions (in which the speaker/writer makes no assumption about whether the condition is being fulfilled) are called **first-class conditions**, contrafactual conditions are called **second-class conditions**, conditions involving the subjunctive (present general and future more vivid) are called **third-class conditions**, and conditions involving the optative (future less vivid) are called **fourth-class conditions**, although this last category does not occur in complete form in the New Testament. In this scheme, it is the mood of the protasis (if clause) that determines the classification. This scheme arises because the optative is so rare in later Greek, and thus the language of that period has lost some of its earlier precision in describing conditional sentences. (For example, it cannot distinguish between future more vivid and future less vivid possibilities.) Table 9-4 (page 169) contains some of the information found in the previous table, but recast into the terms that *koine* Greek grammar books are likely to use.

Table 9-3   Conditional Sentences in Greek

Type of Condition	Verb Form and Conjunction in If-Clause (Protasis)	Verb Form and Particle in Main Clause (Apodosis)
Present Simple ("*If* Paul is here, we are happy.")	εἰ (*ei*) + Present Indicative	Present Indicative
Present General ("*Whenever* Paul is here, we are happy.")	ἐάν (*ean*) + Present Subjunctive	Present Indicative
Present Contrafactual ("If Paul were here, we would be happy.")	εἰ (*ei*) + Imperfect Indicative	Imperfect Indicative + ἄν (*an*)
Past Simple ("*If* Paul was here, we were happy.")	εἰ (*ei*) + Imperfect, Aorist, or Perfect Indicative	Imperfect, Aorist, or Perfect Indicative
Past General ("*Whenever* Paul was here, we were happy.")	εἰ (*ei*) + Aorist Optative	Imperfect Indicative
Past Contrafactual ("If Paul had been here, we would have been happy.")	εἰ (*ei*) + Aorist Indicative	Aorist Indicative + ἄν (*an*)
Future Most Vivid ("If Paul comes [as is very likely], we will be happy.")	εἰ (*ei*) + Future Indicative	Future Indicative
Future More Vivid ("If Paul comes [as is plausible], we will be happy.")	ἐάν (*ean*) + Present Subjunctive	Future Indicative
Future Less Vivid ("If Paul should come [as is unlikely], we would be happy.") ("If Paul comes, we will be happy.")	εἰ (*ei*) + Future Optative	Future Optative + ἄν (*an*) (or Present Subjunctive)

Table 9-4 Greek Conditional Sentences as Classified in Some *Koine* Grammar Books

Type of Condition	Verb Form and Conjunction in If-Clause (Protasis)	Verb Form and Particle in Main Clause (Apodosis)
First Class (in present time) ("*If* Paul is here, we are happy.")	εἰ (*ei*) + Present Indicative	Present Indicative
First Class (in past time) ("*If* Paul was here, we were happy.")	εἰ (*ei*) + Imperfect, Aorist, or Perfect Indicative	Imperfect, Aorist, or Perfect Indicative
First Class (in future time) ("If Paul comes, we will be happy.")	εἰ (*ei*) + Future Indicative	Future Indicative
Second Class (in present time) ("If Paul were here, we would be happy.")	εἰ (*ei*) + Imperfect Indicative	Imperfect Indicative + ἄν (*an*)
Second Class (in past time) ("If Paul had been here, we would have been happy.")	εἰ (*ei*) + Aorist Indicative	Aorist Indicative + ἄν (*an*)
Third Class (in present time) ("*Whenever* Paul is here, we are happy.")	ἐάν (*ean*) + Present Subjunctive	Present Indicative
Third Class (in future time) ("If Paul comes [as is plausible], we will be happy.")	ἐάν (*ean*) + Present Subjunctive	Future Indicative
Fourth Class (in future time) ("If Paul should come [as is unlikely], we would be happy.")	εἰ (*ei*) + Future Optative	Future Optative + ἄν (*an*)

In this chapter we have examined various ways Greek and Latin can express specific conceptual relations of ideas by putting sentences together using subordinate clauses, infinitive phrases, or participial phrases. Of course, the descriptions in this chapter do not remotely exhaust the possibilities for constructing Greek and Latin sentences, but this discussion should have given you a grasp of the different ways to put ideas together, as well as some initial exposure to the specifics of how Greek and Latin sentences are formed. As you progress in your study of one or both classical languages, you may find it useful to return to this chapter and to note the ways the new constructions you are learning fit into this overall framework of Greek or Latin syntax.

In the final chapter of this book, I would like to offer suggestions on how to analyze a complex Greek or Latin sentence, so as to recognize which constructions are actually present and how they combine to express complete thoughts.

APPENDIX: GRAMMATICAL TERMS INTRODUCED IN CHAPTER 9

Ablative absolute: See **Absolute construction**. In Latin, the noun/pronoun and participle of an absolute construction go in the ablative case.

Absolute construction: A construction (consisting of a noun or pronoun, a participle, and perhaps various modifiers) that is grammatically independent of the rest of the sentence (e.g., "The day being rainy, Camden did not go for a run"). See **Ablative absolute**, **Genitive absolute**.

Actual result: An event that follows upon the action of the main clause.

Articular infinitive: In Greek, the use of a neuter definite article with an infinitive. This enables the infinitive to assume the case of the article and thus to be used in a variety of ways.

Causal clause: A subordinate clause that describes an event that causes the action of the main clause (e.g., "Since it was raining, Justin did not play tennis").

Concession: The idea of an adversarial relation between events.

Concessive clause: A subordinate clause that is logically in tension with the main clause (e.g., "Although the court was dry, Justin did not play tennis").

Condition: An event that may or may not have happened, or may or may not happen in the present or the future.

Conditional sentence: A sentence that expresses both a condition and the event that has followed, is following, or will follow should the condition be met.

First-class condition: In some classifications of *koine* Greek grammar, a conditional sentence using the indicative mood. This corresponds to present simple, past simple, and future most vivid conditions in a classical Greek classification scheme.

Fourth-class condition: In some classifications of *koine* Greek grammar, a conditional sentence involving the optative mood. This corresponds to past general and future less vivid conditions in a classical Greek classification scheme.

General condition: In Greek, a conditional sentence that refers not to a particular possibility, but to a more generic, repeatable possibility. Such a condition conveys the idea that "if x ever happens (or 'whenever x happens'), then y happens."

Genitive absolute: See **Absolute construction**. In Greek, the noun/pronoun and participle of an absolute construction go in the genitive case.

Less vivid condition: A conditional sentence in which the speaker/writer assumes the condition is less likely to be fulfilled.

More vivid condition: A conditional sentence in which the speaker/writer assumes the condition is likely to be fulfilled.

Most vivid condition: A conditional sentence in which the speaker/writer assumes the condition is highly likely to be fulfilled.

Natural result: An event that naturally follows the action of the main clause. Natural result usually takes the form of "so . . . that."

Purpose clause: A subordinate clause that expresses the purpose for which the action in the main clause is done (e.g., "The officials dried the court so that Justin might play tennis").

Result clause: A subordinate clause that expresses the result that derives from the main clause's action (e.g., "The officials dried the court, so Justin played tennis").

Second-class condition: In some classifications of *koine* Greek grammar, a conditional sentence using the indicative mood and ἀν (*an*) to express a contrary-to-fact idea. This corresponds to present or past contrafactual conditions in a classical Greek classification scheme.

Simple condition: A conditional sentence in which the speaker/writer makes no assumption about whether the condition has been fulfilled, is being fulfilled, or will be fulfilled.

Temporal clause: A subordinate clause whose relation to the main clause is one of time.

Third-class condition: In some classifications of *koine* Greek grammar, a conditional sentence involving the subjunctive mood. This corresponds to past general and future more vivid conditions in a classical Greek classification scheme.

10

READING A GREEK OR LATIN SENTENCE

Some Suggestions

This book has repeatedly proceeded from function to form, but as you learn Greek or Latin you will find that your book is probably arranged on the basis of the forms you have to learn. Of course, arranging textbooks in order of forms is perfectly logical, and one might argue that there is no other way to do it. Greek and Latin have a very large number of forms, many of which you have to be able to recognize in order to read those languages well. As I have mentioned at various points in this book, the fact that I have not taken that approach stems from two major factors. First, as I mentioned in the introduction, this is a supplement to a textbook, not a substitute for one. Second, I am convinced that understanding the big picture of what any language needs to accomplish is very helpful in enabling you to understand and recognize the various forms and their usages. This second factor in particular has shaped the way I have proceeded in this book.

Now, however, as you look at a complicated Greek or Latin sentence, you have to think both from function to form and from form to function. There are specific words, forms, phrases, and clauses in front of you. It will be hard for you to identify them if you do not focus on form. It will be even harder for you to understand how they fit together if you do not focus on function. At this point, you cannot think merely from function to form (as I have asked you to do throughout this book), or merely from form to function (as your textbook has likely been teaching you to do). You need to be able to think in both directions. Therefore, in this concluding chapter, I will offer some suggestions for thinking both from function to form and from form to function, and thus I will try to help you improve your ability to read complicated sentences in one of the classical languages.

Do Not Pretend You Can Do Something in Your Head If You Cannot

Whenever one is studying a modern foreign language, of course, the goal is to be able to speak, understand, and read that language relatively easily. With an ancient language the corresponding goal is that a person be able to read and understand the language with ease. Of course, that may never have been your goal. You may be taking Greek or Latin just because you have to, or you may be studying a classical language to improve your English or your technical vocabulary, not primarily to be able to read a body of literature in that language. Even if you did and do intend to read literature in Greek and Latin, now is the time to recognize that you are unlikely to be able to do so "in your head," at least not at this point in your study. There is almost never a student who can sight-read complicated Greek or Latin after a year of study, and even after two, three, or more years, the number of students who can sight-read difficult literature is relatively small. In fact, the number of teachers who can sight-read difficult material in those languages is not particularly high. I cannot take *anything* you might hand me in Greek or Latin, glance at it, and translate it accurately, and I have been reading each of those languages for several decades. Your teacher may not be able to do so, either, although he may quite possibly be better at it than I am.

Part of the reason for this, of course, is vocabulary. Think of how many words you know in English. If you are a typical educated adult native-English speaker, you might know 30,000 or 40,000 words. Furthermore, you know words from all walks of life; you know some of the technical vocabulary of many fields, from auto mechanics to politics to religion. Of course, there are certain technical fields whose vocabulary is rarely recognized by anyone other than specialists, but most of us know a wide variety of words from many fields. It is very rare for a non-native speaker to gain that kind of breadth of vocabulary in a foreign tongue, ancient or modern. What you are hoping for is not that you would be able to pick up anything in Greek or Latin and read it easily. Instead, you are hoping to learn enough grammar and enough of the vocabulary of your field (whether it is religion, history, medicine, or law) that you can read material in your own field with some facility. Of course, vocabulary is only part of the problem. Because Greek and Latin are so complex, because there are so many forms that you have to identify and so many ways to put sentences together, even if you know all the words in the sentence you are reading, it is unlikely that you will be able to put those words together in your head to make sense. It takes practice (often years of practice) to get to the point that you can routinely do that.

As a result, you need to recognize that reading a complex sentence in Greek or Latin involves a series of steps, and you should plan on having to write those steps down or type them into a computer file in order to be able to make sense of the sentences. When you first start studying, your sentences are akin to *Britannia est insula* ("Britain is an island"—the first complete sentence I can remember reading in eighth-grade Latin). At that point, you can easily translate in your head, but very quickly the sentences become sufficiently complex that you can no longer do this. You need to take your time, write down the information you gather at each step (or type it on your computer), and then at the end come up with an acceptable understanding of the sentence. As you begin the task of writing/typing all this information, you will recognize that you need a lot of space to do so. Write or type the sentence out in large letters, leaving large spaces between words and multiple spaces between the lines. Later, as you gain more facility, you will be able to do this with less space by doing some of the steps in your head, but for now, leave yourself lots of space. If you are working on paper, you should write with a pencil, since you will likely make mistakes and need to erase fairly often.

Have a Strategy

A complicated Greek or Latin sentence requires that you have a plan for how you are going to analyze it and understand it. The following is a set of steps that I suggest you follow as your strategy for attacking a difficult sentence. Your teacher may suggest a different order for these steps or a somewhat different set of steps altogether, or you may develop your own set of steps. In any case, you need a plan of attack, a strategy.

Look for Finite Verb Forms to Get a Big-Picture View of the Sentence

I think the easiest way to navigate a Latin or Greek sentence is to go from the big picture to the small picture, and then back to the big picture. Remember that some forms (especially in Latin) are potentially ambiguous: the same noun/adjective ending could be used to indicate more than one case/number combination, or the same verb ending could indicate more than one mood/person/number combination. Remember also that a word in a given case could be used in a variety of ways. So if you simply start with the first word and try to identify its form and function, then move to the second word and so forth, you will wind up with several words whose relation to the words around them will not be clear. Instead, I suggest that the first thing to do is to look through the whole sentence, searching for finite verb forms.

Remember that a finite verb form is one that is limited to a particular person, so it has person, number, tense, mood, and voice. (You may want to refer back to Figure 8-1 to make sure you can identify a finite verb form.) How many such forms are there? If you are working on paper, underline them or draw a box around them, or use some other method to identify them clearly. If you are working in a computer file, designate a color to use in highlighting finite verbs. Of these finite verb forms, how many set up independent clauses? (Remember that in most cases, only indicative and imperative verbs define independent clauses, although subjunctive and optative verbs can do so in a few cases.) How many verbs indicate subordinate clauses?

Find the Subjects and Objects for All the
Finite Verb Forms

The first sentences you read in Greek or Latin were simple ones, usually consisting of a subject, a verb, and an object. Now, with a complex sentence in front of you, you still want to look for subject, verb, and object. Once you have identified each finite verb form, ascertain whether there is an expressed subject for it (that is, whether there is a word in the nominative case and the same number as the verb that can be the subject for that verb) or whether the subject is implied ("I," "you," "he/she/it," or "they" included in the verb form itself). Similarly, if a given verb is transitive (or could be transitive) and active in voice, look for a nearby word in the accusative case that could be its object. If you are working on paper, draw arrows or use some other notation to link the subjects, the verbs, and the objects that go together. If you are working in a computer file, choose colors to mark subjects and objects, or use drawing software to draw lines in your file. (Just remember that the way you mark the relations between words is a means to an end, not an end in itself. Do not become so consumed with your marking system that you waste time getting the computer to mark the words.)

At this point, without delving too deeply into the complexities of the sentence, you should already have a fairly clear idea of its structure. You should know where the clauses are, which ones are independent and which are subordinate, and what the subject and object (if there is one) are for each verb/clause. By starting with the big picture, you have given yourself a good chance to decipher the sentence more quickly and successfully.

Identify All Vocabulary and Forms,
Especially Ambiguous Forms

This may be so obvious that it does not need to be stated, but it is absolutely crucial to your understanding of a Greek or Latin sentence that you identify the forms correctly. You already know which words are the subjects, the verbs, and the objects, but you may not know what each of those words means, and in the case of the verbs, you may not have completely identified the forms yet. (For example, you know that a certain verb is third person singular, but you may not be sure about its tense and mood.) Now is the time to complete the process of identification. Write or type the basic usage (meaning) of each word that you know underneath or above that word, and look up the words you do not know so as to learn their basic usages.

Identify the gender, number, and case of all the nouns, pronouns, adjectives, and articles. Pay special attention to places where a form is ambiguous. Could a given noun be either nominative or vocative? Could it be either dative or ablative? (In Latin, these two cases usually have the same form in the plural.) Also, pay close attention to which declension the noun or adjective follows. There are many instances (especially in Latin) where you must know the declension in order to identify the form correctly. When the form is ambiguous, you may already know enough about the sentence's structure to know which of the options is correct, but if not, write or type the possibilities. Having these possibilities in front of you will help you finish putting the sentence together later.

For all the finite verbs, identify the person, number, tense, mood, and voice. For the non-finite verbal forms, write down all the information each form conveys. Participles have person, number, case, tense, and voice. Infinitives have only tense and voice. (Again, I refer you to Figure 8-1, which lists the parsing information for verb forms and gives you a procedure to follow in gathering that information.) Pay careful attention to ambiguous forms and to instances where you have to know which conjugation a verb is before you can identify its form correctly.

For other words, identify the word class (part of speech). Recognize that many of these non-inflected words can be used as more than one part of speech. For example, καί (*kai*) in Greek or *et* in Latin can be either a conjunction ("and") or an adverb ("also"). Some prepositions (such as *cum* in Latin) can also be used as conjunctions. You may already know enough about the sentence's overall structure to decide whether a word is used this way or that way, but if not, write or type the possibilities.

Use the Case Endings to Finish Determining Which Words Could Go with Which Others

From your preliminary look at the sentence as a whole, you know the subjects and objects. Now you need to finish grouping nouns and other words that go with them into phrases and clauses. Look at the case endings, pay attention to prepositions, articles (in Greek), relative pronouns, and other words that mark out phrases and clauses, and then circle groups of words that go together. Or if you are working on a computer, you may want to use underlining or italics at this point, since you have already used different colors to mark verbs, subjects, and objects. As you mark the groups, identify what kind of phrase or clause each one is. Furthermore, draw arrows from one group of words to the word or words to which it pertains. (For example, circle a relative clause, and draw an arrow from that clause to the antecedent.)

As you do this, you will notice that you are easily eliminating some of the ambiguities of the forms. For example, if a word could be either nominative or vocative based on its form, at this stage it should be obvious which one it is, so you can cross out or delete the possibility you have rejected. If ambiguities persist at this point, find a way to indicate which possibilities still remain. For example, if you are working on paper you could draw two dashed arrows to the words a given phrase might modify, if it is not yet clear which of those it does actually modify.

If More Than One Arrangement Is Possible, Write out the Possibilities

If you are not able to make sense of the sentence once you have identified the forms and used symbols (circles, boxes, arrows, as you see fit) to indicate their relations to one another, the reason may be that there is more than one possible arrangement of the elements. In this case, you should write or type two or more rough translations, indicating the different possibilities. Or, if you are really at a loss, you may need to rewrite or retype the Greek or Latin sentence a couple of different ways, putting the words in an order more comparable to English to try to figure out how the elements go together. When my students are stumped in class, one thing I do quite often is to read the Greek or Latin words back to them, not in the order in which they are written, but in the order the students need to follow in English, so that the students can see the relations between them clearly. In fact, sometimes I will read the words to the students one-by-one in English order, letting them translate each word as I read it until they have come up with a rough translation of the sentence. You can do something similar yourself by recasting the sentence in a more English-friendly word order.

Go from a Rough Translation to a Smooth One

Once you are confident that you understand how the sentence works in Greek or Latin, then you are ready to try to put it into good English. I impress upon my students the fact that translation is always a two-step process (although you may eventually get to the point that you can do the first step in your head). First, one renders the sentence into English words, but preserving the relations between the words in Greek or Latin as closely as possible. This is what you should have already done in the previous stages. Then one should mentally set aside the Greek or Latin sentence, get the meaning of that sentence in mind using the rough translation, and ask oneself, "How do we express that idea in English?" The answer to this question leads to the smooth translation. This is the point at which one takes into account the emphasis and the nuance conveyed by the Greek or Latin word order. For example, if a sentence means, "Thomas did not see Jesus," but the way it is written places a great deal of emphasis on "Jesus," then one might recast the sentence in English to read, "the one Thomas did not see was Jesus." This does not follow the grammar of the original, but it says the same thing, while putting the emphasis in the place where the original sentence puts it.

There is a great deal of art involved in writing smooth translations, because doing so requires not only that one understand the Greek or Latin sentence well, but also that one have a good grasp of how one's own language conveys ideas. In fact, it is often said that the biggest problems for translators come not from the language out of which they are translating, but from their own language, the language into which they are translating. As you progress in your study of Greek or Latin, you will increase in your ability not only to catch the nuances of literature in those languages, but also to express those nuances in the ways English is most elegantly able to do.

Recognize That Using Translations Is Not Always Cheating

This suggestion may surprise you, and for that matter, it may irritate your teacher. When I was taking third-semester Attic Greek, we read Plato's *Apology*. Of course, that is an extremely well-known work, and many translations of it are floating around. Even then (spring of 1986—before the Internet era) it was easy for us to get our hands on translations of the passages we were slaving over for our homework. So the teacher expressly forbade us (in writing!) from using translations in preparing our homework. Of course, there were good reasons for her to do that—if we could have looked up "the answers," we would certainly not have slaved away at what was to us very difficult Greek for as many hours each evening as we did. For similar reasons, your teacher may forbid you from using translations.

If you are like most students of the classical languages, though, you are not so much trying to become fluent in those languages as you are trying to get to the point that you can use them. Unless you are going into historical study of the ancient world as I did, you may never have to read anything in Greek or Latin that has never been translated. Given that possibility, once you have put in your time trying to read a document on your own, it will not normally be "cheating" if you consult translations. Your own effort will help you catch nuances that the translations may not convey clearly, and the translations may help you to understand difficult passages or to correct your mistakes. Used properly, translations may be an important part of the process of improving your Greek or Latin. Because of this, in my advanced classes, I assign not only straight translation projects, but also other projects involving different ways of using the languages that a student will be likely to need. For example, I ask students to compare the Greek text of a given New Testament passage with the Vulgate translation and to write down all the significant differences. I ask students to read a document in English, identify the passages that are important enough to study in Greek or Latin, and then go back and work on those passages themselves. I ask students to compare a classical document to its translation and to identify places where they think the translation could be improved. All of these are skills that scholars who work with languages need to possess, but none of them are quite the same as the skill of translation itself.

A Final Word of Encouragement

By the time you get to this point in this book, you are well aware of how complicated and difficult Greek and Latin are. In fact, if your teacher has had you delay reading part 4 until well into your first year of study, at this point you have already been struggling with the many forms for some months now. I told you at the beginning that it would be hard, and by now you know that it is.

At the same time, I hope this book has also shown you that learning Greek or Latin is by no means impossible. It may be an exercise in humility as you find out how little you actually understood the workings of your own language, but it should not be an exercise in futility. Instead, studying Greek or Latin (or both) should be a challenging exercise in discovery. In part 1 of this book, I mentioned that these languages unlock the doors to vast treasures of knowledge—from the literature many of us want to study to the building blocks of Western civilization to the technical vocabularies of many specialized disciplines. Studying Greek or Latin is worth the struggle, because the rewards of that study are so great.

It should also be clear now that the discoveries that come with studying Greek and Latin are greater than what I mentioned in part 1. Fundamentally, these discoveries have to do with language, with communication. Greek or Latin can be a window into the world of how we express ideas. Even if you never reach the point that you can easily use a classical language to read literature important to you, your study of Greek or Latin will make you more conscious of how you think and communicate, and how others do so. That study will make you more attuned to the subtleties and nuances of both logic and communication. It will make you more aware of the need for rigorous thought, speech, and writing. You will be better at using English because you have studied Greek or Latin. My hope is not only that this book will have made the study of a classical language a bit easier for you, but also that it will have helped open the door to the wonders of communication in general, wonders to which Latin and Greek are so well suited to introduce us.

Index

Note: Page numbers in boldface refer to occurrences of a word in the grammatical appendices to the chapters.

grammarian, 4, 33–38, **48**, 61, 79, 93, 103, 106, 111, 117, 121, 142
Greek language: history of, 13–14
Greek people, xxiii, 10, 14, 20–21, 33–35, 38, 75, 82n4, 85–86

Hardy, Thomas, 3–4
Hebrew language, xxiv, 6, 14, 59n1, 71n4, 105n2, 117n2
Homer, 13, 70
Hungarian language, 44n5, 59n1

imperative mood, 18n1, 108, 112t, **114**, 124, 126–28, 176
imperfect aspect, 110, **114**, 117. *See also* on-going action; progressive aspect
imperfect tense, 120t, 122t, 123t, 127, 131, **137**, 141, 157, 159–60, 164t, 166t, 168t, 169t
indefinite article, 34, **47**, 83–85, 87
indefinite aspect, 110, **114**, 117. *See also* simple aspect; unspecified aspect
indefinite pronoun, 93–94, **98**
independent clause, 42, **47**, 124, 128–29, 155, 160, 176
indicative mood, xviii, 108, 112t, **114**, 124–29, 131, 133, 134t, 135, **137–38**, 155, 157, 159–60, 163, 164t, 165–67, 168t, 169t, **171–72**, 176
Indo-European language family, xiii, xvii, 53, 58–66, 73–74, 87, 94, 97, 103, 108, 117, 118t, 119, 125, 150
Indonesian language, 7
infinitive, 113, 134, 136, **137–38**, 139–46, 148–49, 151, **152**, 156–60, 164t, 170, **170**, 178
inflected language, 44, 53, 73, 79, 155. *See also* synthetic language
inflection/inflect, 44–46, **47–49**, 53, 57–58, 60–62, 69, 73, 79, 96, 152, 155, 178. *See also* accidence; morphology
instrumental case/function, 61, 63t, 65–67, 68t, **76**
intensive pronoun, 91, 93, **98**
interjection, 33, 37, 38t, 38–39, **47**

interrogative pronoun, 94, **98**
intransitive verb, 104, **114**
Italian language, 15, 24n4, 44, 59, 87

Jesus Christ, 17, 18, 58, 61–62, 70, 80–81, 86, 88, 96, 126–27, 144, 147, 149, 156–60, 180
John, St., 17, 30, 86, 88, 160
Jude the Obscure, 3

Latin language: history of, 14–15
Latin people, xvi, 35. *See also* Roman people
law, xx–xxi, 3, 16, 21, 24, 73–74, 150, 175
less vivid condition, 165, 166t, 167, 168t, **171**
Lewis, C. S., xxii–xxiii
locative case/function, 62, 63t, 65–67, 68t, **77**

Mary, St., 149
masculine gender, 71–72, **76–77**, 81–83, 87–88, 90, 95–97, 134t, 144
meaning, xxiii, 8, 18–19, 20n2, 21, 23, 26–27, 29, 34, 36, 39, 40, **46–47**, **49**, 62, 69, **77**, 103, 109, **114–15**, 129, **138**, 143–45, **152**, 158, 160, 163, 167, 178, 180. *See also* definition; usage
medicine, xx–xxi, 16, 175
middle voice, 105n2, 106–7, 112t, **114**, 135t, 141–42, 145, 146t, 161
mi verb, 136, **137**
modifier/modify, 34, 36, 40, 42, **46–48**, **76–77**, 80, 82, 86, 95, 144–45, 147, 160–61, **170**, 179. *See also* adjective; adverb; qualifier
mood, 107–9, 112–13, **114–15**, 116, 124–28, 130–33, 135–36, 139, 150–52, 157, 159–60, 164–67, **171–72**, 176, 178
more vivid condition, 165, 166t, 167, 168t, **171–72**
morphology, xviii, 40, **46–48**. *See also* accidence; inflection
most vivid condition, 165, 168t, **171**

Understanding Language: A Guide for Beginning Students of Greek & Latin
was designed and typeset in ScalaPro and Scala Sans display type by
Kachergis Book Design of Pittsboro, North Carolina. It was printed on
55-pound Natural, and bound by Versa Press of East Peoria, Illinois.